KU-126-082

Contents

Contents..

Creating a
Home Page
on the internet

An illustrated step-by-step guide for beginners

Richard Cochrane

www.internet-handbooks.co.uk

First published in 2001 by Internet Handbooks Ltd, Plymbridge House, Estover Road, Plymouth PL6 7PY, United Kingdom.

Customer services tel:	(01752) 202301
Orders fax:	(01752) 202333
Customer services email:	cservs@plymbridge.com
Distributors web site:	www.plymbridge.com
Internet Handbooks web site:	www.internet-handbooks.co.uk

Note: The contents of this book are offered for the purposes of general guidance only and no liability can be accepted for any loss or expense incurred as a result of relying in particular circumstances on statements made in this book. Readers are advised to check the current position with the appropriate authorities before entering into personal arrangements.

Case studies in this book are entirely fictional and any resemblance to real persons or organisations is entirely coincidental.

Printed and bound by The Cromwell Press Ltd, Trowbridge, Wiltshire.

List of illustrations

Illustrations..

If you're reading this book, you probably want to use the amazing world wide web to communicate something to other people. You've probably realised that to communicate effectively, you need to be able to speak as well as listen. Well, that's what this book is here to do: to show you how to become an active creator on the web, not just a consumer.

Presumably, you have used the web already. If not, check that your computer has a modem, and that it is linked to an internet service provider (ISP). Start using the internet regularly. Not doing so would be like trying to make a television programme without any experience of watching television. If you would like some basic help, another title in this series, *Getting Started on the Internet*, should be the answer.

At the time of writing, a modem can cost as little as £10, and connection via an ISP – once a serious financial consideration – is usually free of charge. Installing an internal modem requires some nerve (you have to open the box of your computer and push a printed circuit board into a slot) but it's usually painless, particularly if you buy a well-known brand. The shop which sold you the modem will probably be prepared to install it for you – at a cost – if you're nervous about it. Alternatively, you might prefer to buy an external modem, which is designed to plug into one of the sockets which exists for the purpose (a 'serial port') in the back of your PC.

Installing your ISP's software ought to be very easy – if not, try a different one. ISP disks are available free from many high-street shops and on the front of computer magazines. The best-known ISPs include America Online, CompuServe, Freeserve, BT Internet, Demon and Virgin Net – but there are hundreds to choose from. Just pop the disk into your computer, and follow the on-screen instructions. You will be online in a matter of minutes.

What is the web, exactly?

The world wide web is made up of individual web sites. A web site is a collection of web 'pages' – individual screens – which are displayed on your computer screen one at a time. These pages are linked together to create the particular web site. You can follow (click on) the links to explore what's on the site.

For example, on a site about classic cars, there might be an index page which is linked to pages about specific makes and models, owners' clubs, and manufacturers. Each of these pages will at least be linked to one other page, usually the index page. So you, the user, look at the index page, click on the link which says 'Owners' Clubs', and then read the information about clubs. Then, you click on the link marked 'Index' to take you back to the index page again.

If this was all the world wide web was about, we wouldn't be getting so excited about it, and we wouldn't even call it 'the world wide web'. The thing which makes the web exciting is that these sites are also linked together.

Imagine that the club for owners of vintage Bentleys has its own web site. Well, it's just as easy to link to their 'index' page as it is to link to your own. So the 'Owners' Clubs' page of our classic cars site might contain a link to the Bentley owners' club site, too. This gives rise to the phenomenon of 'surfing'. This means following a trail of links from site to site in search of something specific, something unusual, or just something amusing. That's how the web is supposed to work – by following the links from one place to another. It doesn't sound like much, but this is a revolutionary new way of thinking about the gathering, storing and presentation of truly vast amounts of information.

Why get on the web?

The web is a tool for communicating with people. If you're just reading other people's communications, you're using it passively, like a television or a radio. But the web was never intended to be used passively. It's not the sort of thing you're supposed to sit back and be spoon-fed.

The web is, and always has been, interactive. It's about getting your hands dirty and it's being constantly developed by the very people who use it. Creating web pages, however, has another benefit. It's an excellent way to make contact with people, share information, and develop a network of your own.

This is a useful thing to do whether you are sharpening up your bridge-playing skills or growing a small business. It's also enormous fun, and a very marketable skill in the employment market. The best part is that it's pretty easy, too.

What this book can tell you

This book won't tell you enough to get you a highly paid job as a corporate web designer. There are other books which deal with creating flashy, super-slick sites. This book isn't about that. It's about creating your first web site, with a minimum of effort and technical expertise. You will be able to create a very good-looking site from the basic skills presented in this book, and when you want to move on, those skills will provide a firm foundation.

It explains the basics of HTML, the special language used to create web sites. It tells you how to plan and write your site, and what to consider when organising information and communicating it via the web. It introduces you to some key web design concepts, and gives advice on how to make your site look the way you want it to. It explains how to put your pages together and publish them on the internet where everyone can see them. Then it tells you how to attract visitors to your site and develop a whole online network of people and information. Since you'll be feeling rather at home in the online world by then, we'll end by looking at some more advanced concepts and how to learn more using resources on the web itself.

Please take this book slowly. Read it with the computer in front of you and, above all, experiment. You can't harm your computer by getting any of this wrong, so go ahead and tinker. It's the best way to learn.

Richard Cochrane

richardcochrane@internet-handbooks.co.uk

1 Your first web page

In this chapter we will explore:

▶ *getting the software you need*
▶ *creating a simple web page*
▶ *what are tags?*
▶ *identifying your page as HTML*
▶ *head and body*
▶ *a simple method for working with HTML*
▶ *creating paragraphs*
▶ *using bold and italic*
▶ *setting the font face*
▶ *setting the font size*
▶ *creating line breaks*
▶ *indenting*
▶ *aligning paragraphs*
▶ *a summary of tags*

. . . .

Getting the software you need

Which tools do I need?
This book assumes that you are using a PC (personal computer) running Microsoft Windows 95 or above (e.g. Windows 98 or Windows 2000). However, any computer can be used for making web pages, and the procedures are virtually identical.

If you are using an older system like DOS, you will not be able to have more than one program running at once. You will then find the process much more painful than it needs to be. In that case, consider installing Windows 3.11. This operating system exists alongside DOS, and will run on virtually any PC.

16-bit and 32-bit
Operating systems for the PC tend to come in one of two flavours: 16-bit and 32-bit.

1. 16-bit generally refers to older systems like DOS and Windows 3.11.

2. 32-bit generally refers to modern systems like Windows 95, Windows 98, Windows 2000, and NT4.

16-bit systems don't have as many bells and whistles as 32-bit systems. You will find that some things in this book will work differently under 16-bit systems. If you are using anything more powerful than a rather basic 486 processor with 16 megabytes (Mb) of RAM (random access memory), you should be ideally running a 32-bit system. Older machines, however, may not be able to cope. If you are using a computer manufactured in the last couple of years you should have no problems.

To get started, you will also need two pieces of software:

▶ a browser

▶ a text editor

These are indispensable for web-site creation.

The browser
A browser looks at a web page and displays it for you on the screen. It is very similar to how a word processor displays text documents on the screen. The chances are that you already have a browser, and you may already know how to use it. The two most common browsers are Internet Explorer (from Microsoft) and Navigator (from Netscape).

(a) Internet Explorer comes free with modern versions of Microsoft Windows. You will find it in the Program Files directory, under Internet Explorer. It also comes with most internet connection packages, including the free ones. If you don't have this browser, you can just go to the Microsoft site and download it 'free' (but remember, it's your phone call):

Fig. 1. Microsoft Internet Explorer is the world's most popular web browser. Here it is displaying a page from the Yahoo! web site.

http://www.microsoft.com

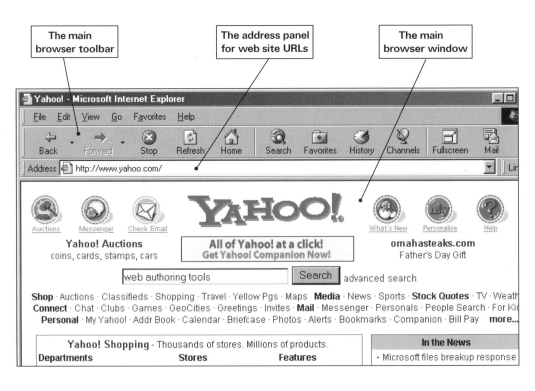

The main browser toolbar

The address panel for web site URLs

The main browser window

(b) Netscape Navigator is a very similar browser to Explorer, though not as popular. Many users prefer one over the other. Both should work equally well on your system. If you would prefer to try Navigator, download it here:

Fig. 2. Netscape Navigator is Microsoft's main competitor in the browser market. Here it is displaying a page from the Yahoo! web site.

http://www.netscape.com

| The main browser toolbar | The address panel for web site URLs | The main browser window |

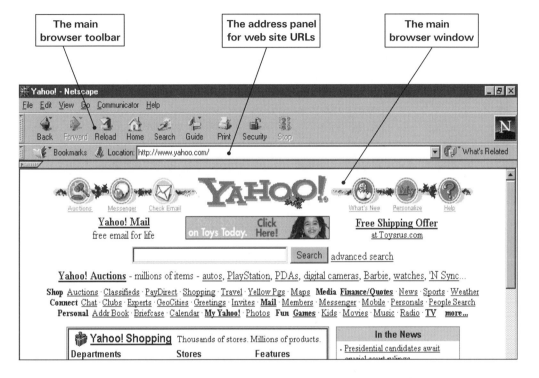

These are big pieces of software, and downloading over a modem line will take a long time. Try to schedule your download for a time when the internet is less busy – early morning for Europe, late evening or night-time for the USA. This will speed things up and minimise your phone bill. Connecting at off-peak times (evenings and weekends) is much cheaper with most telephone companies, too.

These pieces of browser software are also often available on the CD-ROMs which appear free on the front of computer magazines.

Virtually everyone who accesses the world wide web uses one of these two browsers. Everything in this book works exactly the same in both, unless it says otherwise. This is an issue for web designers, because the browsers do tend to display things in different ways. We'll see more on this throughout this book.

A text editor

Fortunately, your computer already has a text editor.

(a) If you are using Windows 3.1, 3.11, 95 or 98 it's called Notepad.

(b) In DOS, just type EDIT and the editor should appear.

(c) On the Apple Mac, the program is called SimpleText.

(d) On UNIX you might like to use EMACS.

If you're using a Mac or UNIX system, though, check the documentation as some of the procedures in this book will work slightly differently.

Fig. 3. Notepad, with some sample text. Notepad is a plain text editor which doesn't allow you to format your documents. This, oddly enough, makes it ideal for creating web sites by writing HTML.

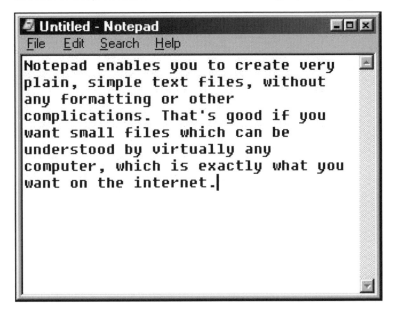

A text editor is like a very primitive word processor. You type in the text and the text editor stores it, without any of the formatting or other information which a program like Microsoft Word adds in. This is very important because web pages need to be plain, clean and simple (you will see why in a moment).

There are programs available which claim to give you a more visual way to create web sites. As a beginner, you should avoid them. The pages they produce are messy and often cause problems, and unless you have a good understanding of HTML you're unlikely to be able to identify and fix them. Start simply, with a text editor, and you'll probably continue to use it in the future. It's quicker and easier in the end, even if these so-called 'what you see is what you get' (WYSIWYG) applications seem appealing at first.

Even companies which design complex web-based software tend to use text editors rather than WYSIWYG software. As a wise man once said, 'Nothing on the market can take an English-language description of what you want and turn it into well-formed code.' It's true. WYSIWYG editors may provide something that looks like good HTML, but you'll almost certainly have to edit that code to make it work properly. You may as well just write it yourself, understanding everything as you go so that fixing problems will be a breeze.

Your questions answered

Can I use a word processor to write my web pages?
Yes, but be sure to save the file as an 'ASCII', 'text only' or 'MS-DOS Text' file, not a word-processor document. Using a simple text editor is recommended because there is less scope for problems.

Why do I need two programs to create my web pages?
It's true that most tasks only require one piece of software, like a spreadsheet or database program. Making web pages isn't like this. We'll need to use one program – the text editor – to create our pages, and a different one – the browser – to look at them.

Creating a simple web page

How HTML works
HTML is a convention which browsers use to display the same information in different situations. You probably know that a word-processed file which you created on your PC wouldn't transfer too well onto your friend's Apple Mac; the web isn't like that – the world wide web has 'cross-platform portability'. This means that it works on virtually any computer. And like anything portable and efficient, web pages have to be lightweight and simple. That's why the information all lives in a plain, old-fashioned text file.

Viewing a text file with a browser
Open your text editor and type a sentence or two. Here's an example:

> Welcome to my web site. My name's Richard, and I'm interested in computers, poetry, jazz and the ancient Japanese game of Go.

Save the file. Let's say we've called it 'example'. Most text editors would like you to call it 'example.txt'. Don't. Call the file 'example.html'. If your operating system won't let you do this – the 16-bit ones don't always – then call it 'example.htm'. The 'html' or 'htm' extension both do exactly the same thing: they tell your computer that this is an HTML file.

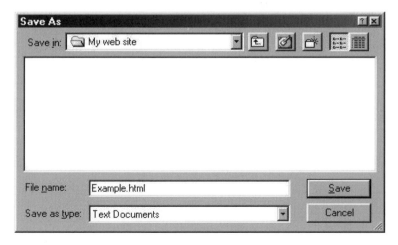

Fig. 4. Using Notepad to save a file with the 'html' extension. This is the first step in telling your computer that you want the file saved as a web document.

Your first web page..

Don't close your text editor, but open up your browser. Click on the File menu and select Open. Now locate the text file you just saved (in Explorer you have to press the Browse button) and open it. In Windows 95 or above, you can just double-click it. The browser will display the file. If it doesn't, you may have to choose Open from the File menu of the browser and search for your file, or type the location of the file, something like 'c:\docs\web\page.html', in the Address field.

Fig. 5. Internet Explorer displaying a simple text file. Without HTML, this is what all web pages would look like.

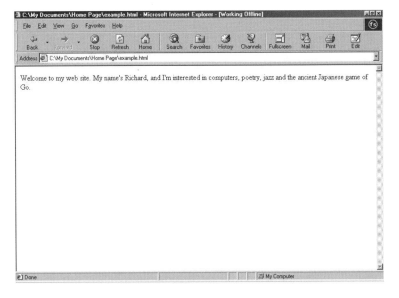

Not very exciting, is it? Well, no. That's because we're looking at a plain text file without any HTML tags in it.

▶ *Tip* – Whenever you're working with web pages, always keep your text editor and your browser open at the same time. In a moment, we'll see a simple method for working with web pages using the two programs at the same time.

If double-clicking an HTML file doesn't open it in your browser under Windows 95 or better, you can do something about it. These procedures aren't difficult, but they are not essential either, so if you'd rather not monkey about with your operating system, or if you're in a hurry, just skip them and go on to the next bit, 'What are tags?'

To get Internet Explorer to automatically open HTML files, do this:

1. In Windows Explorer – not Internet Explorer, but the program you use to look at files on your hard drive – choose Folder Options from the View menu.

2. In the File Types section, find 'Internet Document (HTML)'. It might also be called 'Microsoft HTML document', which might surprise you.

3. Select it and click the Edit button.

4. In the Actions box, you will see a list of things you can do with the file. This is the list which pops up when you right-click on its icon. Select Open, and click Edit.

5. Type in the following settings:

   Application used to perform action:

   > C:\Windows\Explorer.exe /idlist,%l,%L

   (If Internet Explorer isn't in this directory, substitute the path that's right for your PC. You can find this if you don't know it by searching for IEXPLORE.EXE using the Find Files or Folders option under the Start menu.)

   Check 'Use DDE'. Three more options appear.

   DDE message: [ViewFolder('%l','%l',%S)]

   Application: Folders

   Don't put anything under 'DDE Application not running'.

   Topic: AppProperties

6. Click OK, then close the rest of the windows.

Although it looks like a chore, this feature is actually very useful. So useful, in fact, that you might want to set up the following right-mouse-click options while you're at it:

(a) Change the Edit option to use C:\Windows\Notepad.exe. You don't have to use DDE for Notepad, so leave it unchecked. Again, you might have to hunt for the NOTEPAD.EXE file.

(b) If you have Netscape Navigator, you could add an option called something like 'Open in Navigator'. The application to use would be:

C:\Program Files\Netscape\Communicator\Program\netscape.exe

Again, your directory structure might be different. You don't need DDE for this either. If you don't have Navigator yet, you can always come back and do this later.

What are tags?

A simple text file on its own doesn't look very exciting. You've probably seen web sites with colourful graphics, text of different sizes and all manner of other visual elements. Just try to get your text editor to do these things; it won't. It's a stupid, simple, plain text editor. All it knows about are which letters you've typed into it.

That's why you need HTML. HTML stands for 'hyper-text mark-up language'. Don't worry about the first half for now – just think for a moment about the last three words. HTML 'marks up' your plain text with a series of 'tags'. All browsers, wherever they are, can interpret these tags and display the text the way the tags instruct them to.

Identifying your page as HTML

There are a few tags which all web pages should have, so let's start with those. The first one tells the browser that it's looking at a web page, not something else. Here's how it would look in our example page:

```
<html>
Welcome to my web site. My name's Richard, and I'm interested in
computers, jazz and the ancient Japanese game of Go.
</html>
```

There are a couple of things to note here.

1. First, the angle brackets around the tag: <html>. These angle brackets are used to separate tags from ordinary text. As soon as Explorer or Navigator sees an angle bracket, it expects what's inside it to be an HTML instruction, not text which it ought to display.

2. Another thing to notice is the 'closing' tag, </html>. The '/' character indicates you are turning the previous tag off. It might not be too obvious that this is important here, but with other tags it is essential.

▶ *Note:* The <html> tag isn't essential when you're looking at files on your home computer, but the internet is a messy place which, like the real world, is full of nasty surprises. That's why it's best to be cautious and give browsers what they want — even though the most recent versions don't usually need it.

Head and body

An HTML document is divided into two bits: head and body. The head contains information about the document. The body contains the text itself. Here's how to mark up the head and body sections of our web page:

```
<html>
<head>
</head>
<body>
Welcome to my web site. My name's Richard, and I'm interested in
computers, jazz and the ancient Japanese game of Go.
</body>
</html>
```

You can put as much or as little as you like in the head part of the file — it's completely up to you. We'll see what kinds of things you might want to put in there later. Here is just one tag which is very common indeed, and which is usually put in the head section:

< head >
< title > My Home Page < /title >
< /head >

You'll see what the < title > tag does in a moment, but notice that we've turned it off at the end of the title – otherwise the page wouldn't display properly at all. That's one reason why it's a good discipline to always turn off tags even when it doesn't have any obvious effect. It keeps your pages clean and easy to understand for all different kinds of users. Obviously, you can put whatever title you want between the < title > and < /title > tags, so go ahead and be more imaginative than I was.

Fig. 6. Internet Explorer's Refresh button and Netscape Navigator's Reload button do the same job. They update the page you are viewing with any changes that have taken place since it was last loaded up.

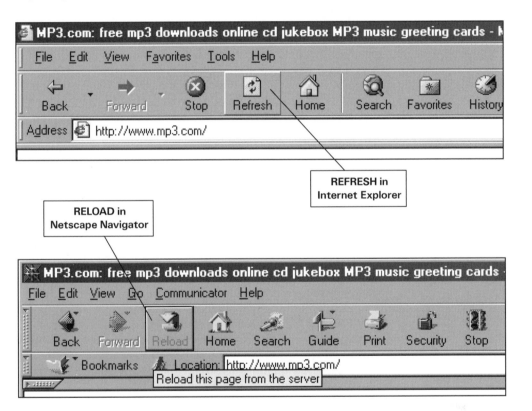

REFRESH in
Internet Explorer

RELOAD in
Netscape Navigator

Reload this page from the server

Now, save the page (yes, it's now a web page); you don't need to use Save As, just save it with the same name as before. Next, have a look at your browser. The page doesn't look any different, does it? Well, click the Refresh button (or in Navigator, the Reload button); this re-loads the page. You'll notice that the very top of the window – the bar where the name of the application usually is – now contains your title.

Fig. 7. This is how the title text appears in the very top section of the browser window.

My Home Page - Microsoft Internet Explorer - [Working Offline]

File   Edit   View   Go   Favorites   Help

Your first web page..

A simple method for working with HTML

The method we've just seen is probably the simplest way to create web pages on your computer. Here it is in summary form:

1. Open your browser and text editor.
2. Create or edit a page using the text editor.
3. View the page by opening it in the browser.
4. Switch back to the text editor to make any amendments.
5. Save the file with the same name.
6. Switch back to the browser and click Refresh or Reload to see your changes.

Creating paragraphs

Now, switch back to your text editor and try typing some more text into the body of the page, maybe like this:

```
<body>
Welcome to my web site. My name's Richard, and I'm interested in computers, jazz, poetry and the ancient Japanese game of Go.

On this site, you can find advice on creating good HTML, links to my music journalism online and information on playing Go over the internet.
</body>
```

Save and then go back to your browser and hit Refresh again. It doubtless looked something like this:

Welcome to my web site. My name's Richard, and I'm interested in computers, jazz, poetry and the ancient Japanese game of Go. On this site, you can find advice on creating good HTML, links to my music journalism online and information on playing Go over the internet.

Why? Simple – HTML doesn't recognise 'hard returns' (the line spaces you put in using the 'return' or 'enter' key to separate one paragraph from another). Instead, browsers expect to see your text broken up into paragraphs, using the <p> tag:

```
<body>
<p>Welcome to my web site. My name's Richard, and I'm interested in computers, jazz and the ancient Japanese game of Go. </p>

<p>On this site, you can find advice on creating good HTML, links to my music journalism online and information on playing Go over the internet. </p>
</body>
```

Save it, go back to your browser and refresh – better?

There are other, more clumsy ways to get the same effect, but using the <p> tag (and others like it) isn't just a matter of coding style. There are people out there using all kinds of weird ways to access the web. The word on the web at the time of writing is that these are only going to get more common as mobile phones and other non-PC gizmos start accessing information online. Although some web creators have chosen not to bother with the closing </p> tag and have mostly got away with it so far, that's not going to last forever. Get on the bus from the start with the strict HTML style we'll use throughout this book. It's a lot better than having to rewrite your entire web site some time in the future.

Using bold and italic

One thing you probably noticed is that this page still doesn't look much like those flashy corporate sites with graphics and colours and suchlike. Well, that's going to take some time, but you can improve the look of even this really simple page.

It's easy to mark text up in bold or italic. Just use <b> for bold or <i> for italics, as in this example:

<p> On this site, you can find advice on creating <i>good</i> HTML, links to my music journalism online and information on <b> <i>playing</i> Go over the internet<b/>.</p>

Here, the word 'good' will appear in italics, 'Go over the internet' will be in bold, and 'playing' will be in bold and italics. It's sometimes a good idea to mark up headings in bold. It would probably be worth taking a moment to tinker with these tags until you're happy with them: you'll be seeing quite a lot more like them as you work through this book.

▶ *Note* – The text-formatting tags used in the rest of this chapter are very common on the web, and they're a good place to get started with HTML. Many of them are, however, officially 'deprecated' in favour of something called 'style sheets', which means that future browsers may not bother to support them. Style sheets are a lot more complicated but also more flexible. Unfortunately, older browsers can't understand them so, at the time of writing at least, these types of tags are still needed. In reality, future browsers will support these tags; if they didn't, they would be unable to properly display the millions of web pages which use these tags.

Setting the font face

The font your browser uses to display this page is the 'default font'. This is probably Times New Roman, because you haven't told it to do anything different. If you want users to see your text in a different font, you will have to 'mark up' the text using the <font> tag. It looks like this:

<font face='Arial'> Welcome </font>

Your first web page...

There's something new here, as you can probably see. The <font> tag can have a number of parameters which you can choose to set the values for. One of these parameters is 'face', which determines the typeface the browser will try to use to display your text. I say 'try' because, if your reader's computer doesn't have the font you specify, the browser will just use the default font anyway. To get around this, you can provide alternatives:

<font face='Arial, Helvetica'> Welcome </font>

Fig. 8. An example of a site which uses Arial as its main font, with bold and varying sizes.

When it encounters this tag, the browser will look for a font called Arial. If it can't find it, it will try to use Helvetica instead. Only if neither of these is present will it resort to the default font.

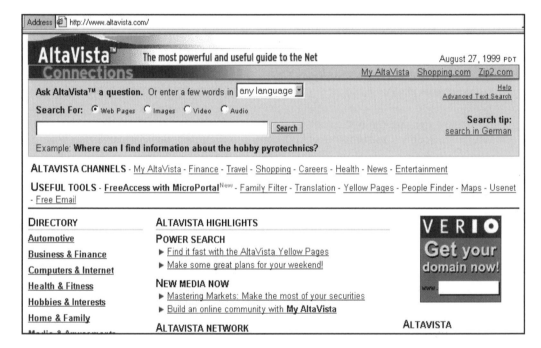

▶ *Tip* – If you use exotic or unusual fonts, always be sure to provide a common alternative, otherwise most people will just see the default font. Browsers interpret what you give them and do the best they can with it; they don't produce identical results every time. That flexibility is part of the strength of the hypertext system and there's no point fighting it too hard.

▶ *Tip* – Arial is available on all Windows PCs. Helvetica comes as standard with the Mac and looks very similar. So this pair of fonts pretty much ensures that everyone will see what you intended if you want this style of typeface.

Setting the font size

You can also set the size of the font simply by doing this:

```
<font size='2'>Welcome </font>
```

Size 2 is a readable, average size for text; 4 or 5 are good for headings, 1 is best for 'small print' only.

Different computers will display these sizes differently, depending on the screen resolution available, but 3 will always be bigger than 2 and smaller than 4.

Let's try turning 'Welcome to my web site' into a heading by setting it in a paragraph on its own, and giving it a larger size. Look carefully at all of these tags:

```
<body>
<font face = 'Arial, Helvetica'>
<p><font size = '4'>Welcome to my web site. </font></p>

<font size='2'>
<p>My name's Richard, and I'm interested in computers, jazz and the ancient Japanese game of Go.</p>

<p>On this site, you can find advice on creating good HTML, links to my music journalism online and information on playing Go over the internet.</p>
</font>
</font>
</body>
```

Let's see how each tag is turned off. The first </font> tag turns off the most recent <font> tag, which in this case set the size to '4'. That's why we need the last </font> tag, which turns off the <font face = 'Arial, Helvetica'> tag from the very beginning of the <body> section.

Now do something similar with your own page, and look at the results by saving and then using the 'Refresh' button on your browser to see the effect. Try playing around with different font faces and sizes until it feels comfortable.

▶ *Tip* – If you wanted to, you could use a single tag to set more than one parameter, like this: <font face='Arial' size='2'> The drawback is that the </font> tag will turn off both the face and the size you've set. It might be worth using if you want exactly the same face and size for all of the text on your page, but it has no real benefits. We'll see some other tags which can do this in a more useful way soon.

Creating line breaks

You probably noticed that HTML paragraphs are separated by a blank line; the lines would otherwise just run to the edge of the screen and then continue in a block. You don't always want that. For example, in the case of a list you might want it to appear like this:

> On this site, you can find:
> 1. advice on creating good HTML
> 2. links to my music journalism online
> 3. information on playing Go over the internet.

Here the list lines are not separated by blank lines, so making each one a separate paragraph won't work (try it). To get this effect, you would use the < br / > tag to insert the line breaks you need. Inserting < br / > is just like hitting the return key once. You could do it like this:

< p > On this site, you can find: < br / > < br / > advice on creating good HTML < br / > links to my music journalism online < br / > information on playing Go over the internet. < /p >

Notice that < br / > is a very unusual kind of tag, because it doesn't need to be closed with a < /br >. For the curious, < br / > is a tag which closes itself – that '/' at the end tells the browser to close the tag immediately. You don't need the '/' right now because all browsers will accept < br > on its own. However, the newest browsing technology will require it, and you might as well be ready. Again, this tiny change keeps your HTML strictly accurate. It means that changes in how the web is accessed won't mean you have to spend whole weekends re-coding your enormous web site in six months' time. Everyone knows that the internet changes fast and that you've got to be ready for it if you're not going to be left behind – even if your site is about the Boer War.

Indenting

You might like to indent the list we just created to make it a bit prettier. You can do this really easily using the < blockquote > tag:

< p > On this site, you can find:
< blockquote > < br / > < br / > advice on creating good HTML < br / > links to my music journalism online < br / > information on playing Go over the internet. < /blockquote > < /p >

This use of < blockquote > doesn't give you any control over how much the lines are indented, but at least it's quick and easy.

View this in your browser, though, and you'll see that more line breaks have appeared. That's because < blockquote > automatically puts two line breaks in for you. So you should remove the < br / > < br / > which are immediately after it. Here's how the paragraph should look:

< p > On this site, you can find:
< blockquote > advice on creating good HTML < br / > links to my music journalism online < br / > information on playing Go over the internet. < /blockquote > < /p >

File Edit View Go Favorites Help

Back Forward Stop Refresh Home Search Favorites History Channels Fullscreen

Address C:\My Documents\Home Page\example.html

Welcome to my web site.

My name's Richard, and I'm interested in computers, jazz and the ancient Japanese game of Go.

On this site, you can find:

> advice on creating good HTML
> links to my music journalism online
> information on playing Go over the internet.

Once more, try creating different lists using the <p>, <br /> and <blockquote> tags. Although it looks quite complicated, it isn't, once you get used to it.

▶ *Tip* – We've already seen that your browser ignores the line spaces you create by hitting the return key. So you can use them as often as you like, to break up the text and make it easier to read:

<p> On this site, you can find:

<blockquote> advice on creating good HTML
links to my music journalism online
information on playing Go over the internet. </blockquote> </p>

This will help you when you come to play around with your web pages at a later date.

Fig. 9. The example page showing use of various formatting tags. This is starting to look more like a real web page.

Aligning paragraphs

At the moment, your browser is displaying all your text flush with the left-hand side of the page – 'left aligned' or 'left justified'. That's the default way to display a paragraph, but you can change it by setting the 'align' parameter of the <p> tag:

<p align='center'> <font size = '4'>Welcome to my web site. </font> </p>

Notice the American spelling of 'center'. You can also specify <p align='right'>.

What now?
That's the basics of presenting your text as an HTML document. Now

you know how to create individual web pages; although they won't yet look that exciting, you can have some fun experimenting with these tags. Try creating pages with different combinations of alignment, indentation, font faces and sizes, bold and italic and so on.

Rather than giving you more tags to learn, the next chapter talks about generating text to put into your web site, so you can experiment with these basic tools while you work through it.

Summary of tags

Here is a quick-reference summary of the tags in this chapter. The first three are 'structural' tags, the rest directly affect the appearance of the page.

Tag	Description
<html>	Should go at the start of every web page.
<head>	Defines the head section of the page.
<body>	Defines the main section of the web page.
<title>	Sets the text which appears at the top of the screen.
<p>	Defines a paragraph; can be used with the 'align' parameter.
<font>	Used with the 'face' and 'size' parameters.
 	Inserts a line break.
<b>	Sets the text in bold.
<i>	Sets the text in italics.
<blockquote>	Indents the text by the default amount.

All these need to be turned off, except the <br /> tag. Tags are turned off by repeating the tag and including a '/' character, e.g. </p>.

2 Organising your content

In this chapter we will explore:

▶ *developing a theme for your web site*
▶ *brainstorming*
▶ *identifying a subject*
▶ *thinking of subject categories*
▶ *filling in the blanks*
▶ *writing specifically for the web*
▶ *starting small*

. . . .

Developing a theme for your web site

What is 'content'?

'Content' refers to all the stuff which is found on a particular web site. It includes graphics, sounds and moving images, but the most important element of content is still the written word. So, although you may not yet know how to insert the more flashy elements into a web page, you can start thinking about the text you want to put on your site.

You may already have an idea of what you want to publish – perhaps a brochure, an article, or even a novel which you have already written. More likely, though, you have an idea of what your site will be about, but nothing on paper as yet. That's fine; in fact, in many ways, that may be a better way to begin. All your content can then be tailor-made for a new web site.

▶ *Tip 1* – Take a critical look at a selection of other people's website content on the web. Get an idea of the kind of things you like and the things you don't. Make a special note of the sites whose text you want to read and those you just flick through. Those you spend time with are almost certainly better written than the rest.

▶ *Tip 2* – While doing this, experiment with setting out your own text on HTML pages. Do this both for practice and as a chance to see your ideas in action.

Brainstorming

If you are creating content from scratch, here is a suggested approach:

1. Identify a subject.

2. Break it down into some possible categories.

3. Fill in the blanks.

You might prefer to do this away from your computer. Some people find their creativity dries up while staring at a screen. Brainstorming often benefits from being a messy process. Spread out blank pieces of paper and scrawl all over them in felt pen, if you like. You're being creative, and you should feel free to do whatever releases your imagination and allows it to run wild.

Identifying a subject

The first thing to be aware of is that your site needs an identity. It should be about something specific, like playing the recorder, your pottery company or Hinduism, for example. If you're not sure about this, start here. Try to sum up what your site is about with one or two key words.

The reason we're doing this is to avoid those terrible 'personal home pages' which have no real structure and precious little content. Really, these are descriptions of the person who created them, and they usually start something like this:

> Welcome to my web site. My name's Richard, and I'm interested in computers, jazz, poetry and the ancient Japanese game of Go.
>
> On this site, you can find advice on creating good HTML, links to my music journalism online and information on playing Go over the internet.

This is not only a helpful example of how to format your page, it's a good example of how *not* to organise your content.

Meeting an information need
The reason is that people generally use the internet to look for something specific. Remember, being online costs people time and money. If they share my interest in Go, they will immediately know from looking at this page that there's probably not very much about the subject here. If I had a lot to say about playing Go on the internet, I'd have a web site about it. What this page says is, 'This site contains a few bits and pieces about various unrelated subjects, and if you want anything useful you're probably better off looking somewhere else'.

Ego advertising
Few people – except celebrities – will be able to attract readers with a web site which is essentially nothing more than an advertisement for their own personality. Have you noticed how many sites like this have a picture of their creator on the front page? If you've been using the web for a while, you probably know that this type of page is an instant turn-off.

The advantage of focus
If you want to create a really good web site, focus on just one interest and make sure that all your content is relevant to it. You can always create a second – and even a third – site if you have that many things you want to tell the world about.

Your web site name and description

To identify your subject completely, give your web site a name and a short description. My music site is called 'musings' – because it contained my own 'musings' about the kinds of music I'm interested in. I described it as: 'An online resource for non-standard musics'. 'Non-standard' kept it open enough that I could cover a lot of different kinds of music, but made it specific enough that you knew immediately you wouldn't find much pop or country and western there.

Fig. 10. Here is a good example of a themed home page.

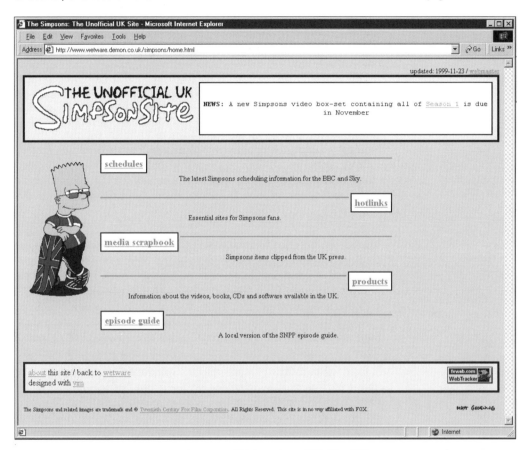

You don't have to keep the name you choose now, but giving the site a name will definitely help you to focus your energies. For example, if you are into the Simpsons television show, don't call it 'Martha's Home Page', call it 'Martha's Simpson's Fan Page'. You can give it a funky name like 'The Duff Blimp' later, if you like. See how, already, 'Martha's Simpsons Fan Page' isn't going to have room for Martha's latest nature poems or a list of her GCSE results? Well, then it's working already.

Thinking of subject categories

Web sites are usually organised into groups of pages. Let's change tack and say we are preparing a web site about your work as a painter. Maybe you can see it breaking down into these sections:

Organising your content ....

- ▶ How I paint
- ▶ Subjects I like to paint
- ▶ Painters I admire
- ▶ Examples of my work
- ▶ Exhibitions I've been in

Obviously, this site will work best once you are able to insert some graphics. Until then, concentrate on how everything will be organised. In any case, it's never the right approach to start with a disk full of graphics files, and then try to structure your site around them.

These categories give just a rough framework of what's going to be on the web site. The first two categories might appear on a single page, or each one might cover several different pages. Don't get tied down as to how it will look in reality. Just use your categories to map out the kinds of things you want to put on your web site.

Keep in mind the two rules of brainstorming:

1. Include everything …

2. … but edit the results.

In other words, don't limit yourself in any way during your brainstorming session. Just write down everything you can think of. Then, when you've harvested as many ideas as you can, go through the list and pick out what you actually want. Keep focused: make sure these categories fit in with your title and your short description of what you want your site to do.

This is only brainstorming. You are not tied to any of this. Later, you can completely reorganise it. What you're trying to do is establish a sense of what kind of things are going to be on the site, and what kind of identity the site could have.

Filling in the blanks

At this stage, you can do as much or as little of this as you want. You might feel inspired to write pages and pages about each category. Or you might prefer to sketch in your ideas about what could go where, and wait a while before you start to rattle the keyboard.

In part, it depends on your approach to writing. Some people like to think their ideas out by writing thousands of words. Often the results aren't much good, but useful ideas will be buried in there somewhere. Other people find writing a chore, and only tackle it once they have a clear idea of their aims. If that's you, make notes instead.

Whichever approach you take – and there's no reason why you shouldn't try both – remember that what you're doing is making notes. Your aim is to clarify your ideas about what will eventually appear on your web pages.

Generating textual content

Writing for the web
Now it's time to think about writing the text which will appear on your web site. It's here that the real fun begins (once you've tidied up the bits of paper and the felt tips). To write for your web site, you'll want to create several pieces of text for each category, if you can. Don't worry about joining them together too much. Just write down the information, descriptions, stories or whatever you want to put there.

▶ *Tip* – Create a folder to save all these pages in. It will make it easier to find them on your computer later. It will also help when you come to finally assemble your site.

Instead of using your word processor to write your text, use a text editor. You can then play around with HTML tags at the same time. Don't worry if all your pages look rather alike – we'll explore the possibilities of page design in the next chapter. Just have fun.

▶ *Tip* – If you have trouble with spelling, type into a word processor which checks your spelling first. Then copy and paste the corrected text into your text editor.

Before you get started, here are a few pointers to help you avoid some common mistakes.

Writing specifically for the web

Most writing on the web is what journalists refer to as 'punchy'. In other words:

1. it uses short sentences and simple words.
2. paragraphs and 'articles' are mostly quite short.

The web as a global medium
Does this mean 'writing for people who are a bit stupid'? No. For a start, remember that the internet is a global medium. That means that many – perhaps most – of your visitors will not have English as their first language. The more restricted your vocabulary, and the simpler your grammar, the more potential readers you will have. The internet aims to make information available on a global scale. Writing like a nineteenth-century academic won't help you there. Besides, have you ever noticed that intelligent people are often very clear communicators?

Technical content
Of course, this doesn't apply to technical vocabulary. If you have a specialist interest like hang-glider design then you're bound to use some specialist terminology along the way. But think twice about choosing an obscure word when an everyday one would do, or about writing a long, complex sentence that could be broken up into two or three simpler ones.

Address 🔗 http://news.ft.com/ft/gx.cgi/ftc?pagename=View&c=Article&cid=FT3GL0CB07C&live=true ▼ 🔗 Go | Link

Plane common sense.

JERSEY EUROPEAN

FT.com
FINANCIAL TIMES

SEARCH
Browse our **Business Directory**

VIEW NAVIGATION →   PERSONAL OFFICE ←

company view
Enter a company...
⦿ Name ○ Symbol
[   ] GO▶

SIGN UP NOW

industry view
Select Industry ▼

US sports coverage @FT.com
click here

Set up your free FT e-mail now
CLICK HERE

US Presidential Elections
All the facts click here

FT Your Money
The essential UK site for making more of your money

Subscribe to the Financial Times Newspaper

Register
Edit your profile

NEWS & ANALYSIS | MARKET NEWS

Talking Stock: Correction or bear market?
By Philip Coggan
Published: April 13 2000 11:48GMT | Last Updated: April 13 2000 12:14GMT

Philip Coggan

With Nasdaq still under the cosh, it's worth talking about some stock market terminology.

For a start, it's easy for those of us who have been following the stock market for a while to get confused by numbers. On Black Monday in October 1987, the Dow Jones Industrial Average fell 508 points. That drop has been beaten in points terms since then and a 300 point drop still looks alarming.

But the key is to concentrate on the percentage change. The Dow's Black Monday drop was 22 per cent. One would need to see the average fall around 2,500 points in current conditions to achieve the same scale.

Market terminology is defined in percentage terms. A fall of 10 per cent is known as a *correction*. Rather like a bad cold, this is unpleasant at the time but you can be confident of recovery.

A *bear market* is a much more serious business. There is no official definition but it is clear that the market needs to fall at least 25 per cent and, even more importantly, to stay down for a period of years. On that definition, we have not had a real bear market since the 1970s.

What we have had since then are a number of declines of 20 per cent or more which seemed serious at the time but merely turned out to be a passing phase. The period around Black Monday turned out to fall into this category as did the Russian/hedge fund crisis of 1998.

market view
News & Analysis ▼
Premium Research ▼
Market Prices ▼

forums
Tesco and e-retail
Martin Wolf on globalisation
Is Microsoft doomed?
Taiwan's future
Sports & broadcasting
Internet start-ups
Endorsing Vladimir Putin

columnists
Comment: Bear baiting
Baker: Where the buck stops
Coggan: Talking stock
Stephens: Against the world
View: Brutish and long
The Lex Column
Recent columnists

special reports
European E-business Review
Budget 2000
FT Euro
US Elections
Connectis e-Vol 2
World's Most Respected
World Economy & Finance
World Trade Organization
Davos 2000

Fig. 11. Short paragraphs and punchy sentences read better on a computer screen than long flowing lines of prose. That doesn't mean that what you write can't be intelligent.

Reading from a computer screen
The reason for keeping paragraphs and articles short is slightly different. The fact is, nobody likes reading large lumps of text from a screen. If you've ever tried it, you probably found that after a while you developed a headache or eye strain. People still prefer paper for most reading. Of course, you can print out a web page if you want to, but how often do you bother? Isn't it more typical that you read the first couple of paragraphs and then move on?

With the world wide web, nobody has a captive audience. If you bore your readers, you will quickly lose them. Make your information as accessible as possible by keeping it short and to the point.

Writing and editing
To achieve this kind of writing style, apply the same rule as for brainstorming. Write what you like, and then edit it later. Make sure you don't repeat yourself unnecessarily. Simplify your language as far as you can. Of course, some sites need a different approach (literary ones, for example) but most web pages benefit from a much tighter, more disciplined writing

style than would be used for paper communications. Here are three practical tips:

▶ *The screen area* – When you write your first pieces of content, make them no more than one screen long. That will help you get a feel for what's about right on a web page, and also stop you wasting your time writing something long which you might throw away later.

▶ *Preview* – Look at each page as you finish it in your browser. Would you read all of this? What if the font was larger or smaller? The only way to get a feel for this is to view it on-screen.

▶ *Headings* – Give each piece you write a heading, and stick to the subject in the heading. That will help keep you focused on the subject in hand. If you think of something to write that doesn't fit the title, create a separate file and a separate heading.

Starting small

It makes sense not to write more than a dozen of these pages at this stage. You'll want to create a design for your pages and learn a few other things before you go online. If you start off with a hundred pages you will only create a lot more work for yourself.

You'll probably want to start your site with one or two pages for each category. That will give you a feel for the content you want to present to your readers – and that's all you need to get started. As we work through the next two chapters, in which we'll be learning a whole host of new HTML tags, you'll probably keep thinking of new ideas for content.

The brain is like that. Make it concentrate on design – as we're about to in the next chapter – and it will immediately want to consider the text that goes inside it. Don't fight this instinctive process. Keep notes of ideas as they occur to you.

Remember, until you actually publish, everything remains 'work in progress'. If you have second thoughts, you can change anything you want.

3 Creating colours and graphics

In this chapter we will explore:

▶ *simplicity for good web design*
▶ *how colour works on the web*
▶ *getting a colour picker*
▶ *web safe colours*
▶ *DIY hexadecimal colours*
▶ *setting a background colour*
▶ *setting text colours*
▶ *creating graphics on the web*
▶ *downloading graphics*
▶ *creating your own graphics*
▶ *picking the right graphics format*
▶ *placing a graphic on your page*
▶ *controlling image size*
▶ *transparency*
▶ *using a graphic as a background*
▶ *degradable design: the 'alt' parameter*

Simplicity for good web design

If you've followed the advice in the previous chapters, you should now have a handful of web pages. Maybe they display your text using bold and italics, paragraphs, different font sizes and faces, block-quotes, line breaks and different alignments.

In this chapter, and the next, we'll add in the tags which will turn these simple text-based pages into colourful ones, with the kinds of graphics and layouts you see on professional sites. Once you've got through it all, the only limit to the effects you can produce will be your own imagination.

Talk to any designer, and the chances are their top design value will be simplicity, especially if the design involves text and material published on the internet. It's easy to use the tags in this chapter to create an ugly, over-complicated mess. Good web sites avoid that. By thinking about design carefully, their creators put together pages that are simple, clear and good-looking.

How colour works on the web

One thing you might have noticed about your web pages is that they are all in black and white – black text on a white background. Wouldn't it be more fun to have coloured text and a coloured background, like so many web sites?

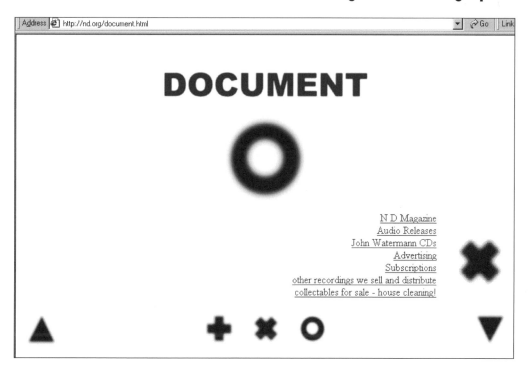

Address | http://nd.org/document.html | Go | Link

Let's start by setting the background colour for the page. First, open up one of your web pages. Now change the <body> tag so that it reads as follows:

    <body bgcolor='green'>

Save the file, and look at it in your browser. Hey presto: a green background. Notice the American spelling of colour as 'color' – spell it the British way and your browser won't understand.

RGB colours

That's all well and good if you want one of the basic colours which browsers recognise, e.g. orange, brown, red, blue, green, pink, purple, beige, cyan, yellow, black and white. There are quite a lot of them; you can find a list at the Microsoft and Netscape sites:

    http://www.microsoft.com
    http://www.netscape.com

If one of these colours suits your needs exactly, that's fine. The chances are, though, that you will want to invent your own colours because the ones mentioned above are just the basic, general-purpose ones. If you want a subtle shade of vermilion, forget about using these standard colours.

Colour on the web works on the RGB model. RGB stands for red, green, blue. Basically, you tell the browser how to mix its paint from

Fig. 12. The ND web site may look simple – even crude – but that's one of its strengths. It has a strong identity and loads quickly. Its only downside is that these cryptic symbols, cool though they look, make navigating the site a matter of trial and error.

Creating colours and graphics......................................

these three pots. You can get any colour imaginable if you know how to mix them up. The result is a tag something like this:

```
<body bgcolor='#2364FD'>
```

What does this mean? It says: make a colour from 23 parts red paint, 64 parts green paint and FD parts blue paint.

FD parts? The web, rather irritatingly, uses a hexadecimal numbering system, which uses the letters A to F as well as the digits 1 to 9. That's why, unless you understand hexadecimal, it's a good idea to use a colour picker to help you.

Getting a colour picker

The easiest way to create colours for your HTML documents is to get one of the various colour pickers available. These are small pieces of software which will tell you the RGB number for any colour you choose. Here are some places to find colour pickers for Windows 95/98:

http://topsoft.com/main/4035/14775484.asp

http://www.longship.demon.co.uk/colorpik

htm http://gamma.nic.fi/~spruce/pmcp/index.htm

All three have simple red, green and blue sliders to enable you to find the exact colour you want. Once you have found it, the colour picker tells you which code to use in your web page. All are very easy to use. WebPalette (the first one on this list) is recommended for Windows 95/98/2000. If you use a different type of system, you will still find lots of suitable colour pickers online.

'Web safe' colours

Some colours are considered safer for use on the web than others. These are colours which will look the same on most people's computers, even if they have an older style of monitor. There are 216 colours which are considered safe. WebPalette (see above) provides access to these. You can also see an online palette of safe web colours here at the WebTorch web site:

http://www.webtorch.com/download/websafe.htm

Ideally, you should stick to using these 'safe' colours, but you can use another colour if none of these looks quite right for your purposes. Just remember that, if you do this, some of your readers might not see what you intended.

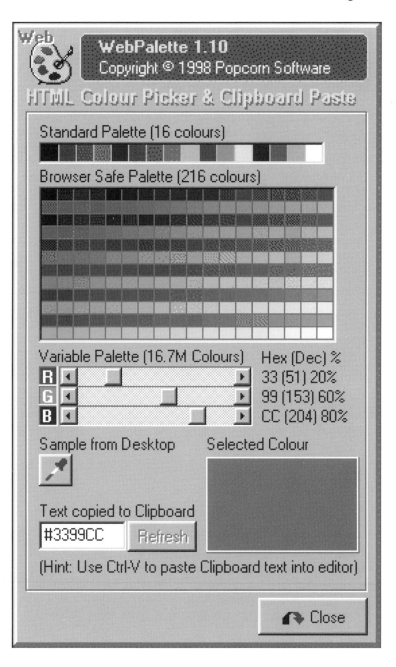

Fig. 13. WebPalette is a colour picker. It enables you to choose the colour you want and see the RGB code for it. You can then just paste the code into your web pages at the right points to achieve exactly the colour you want.

DIY hexadecimal colours

You can also invent your own colours. To do this, it is helpful to learn to count in hexadecimal – which will also make you look like a real computer geek. It's not difficult. Forget about converting these numbers into ordinary ones; that's not important for our purposes.

Creating colours and graphics.....................................

Pick the hex value of any colour from the chart and enter it into your tag, e.g. for a black background : BODY BGCOLOR="#000000"

"#000000"	"#000033"	"#000066"	"#000099"	"#0000CC"
"#330000"	"#330033"	"#330066"	"#330099"	"#3300CC"
"#660000"	"#660033"	"#660066"	"#660099"	"#6600CC"
"#990000"	"#990033"	"#990066"	"#990099"	"#9900CC"
"#CC0000"	"#CC0033"	"#CC0066"	"#CC0099"	"#CC00CC"
"#FF0000"	"#FF0033"	"#FF0066"	"#FF0099"	"#FF00CC"
"#003300"	"#003333"	"#003366"	"#003399"	"#0033CC"
"#333300"	"#333333"	"#333366"	"#333399"	"#3333CC"

Fig. 14. WebSafe is one of many sites that show the 'safe' web colours and their codes in a simple and very effective way. You may find it useful to save a page like this onto your hard disk, for future reference.

This section might be interesting to you, or not. It's far from essential. If it gives you a headache, skip it.

Counting up to nine in hexadecimal is easy:

1 2 3 4 5 6 7 8 9

It is just like the familiar decimal system. But look what happens after that:

1 2 3 4 5 6 7 8 9 A B C D E F

The numbers 10 to 15 are written using letters, not numbers. Now look what happens:

1 2 3 4 5 6 7 8 9 A B C D E F 10 11 12

So '10' in hexadecimal is actually the number 16. Confused yet? Don't be. Just remember that F is bigger than E, but less than 10. It helps if you think of the hexadecimal number '10' as 'one-nought', not 'ten'. Here's what happens after 12 ('one-two'):

12 13 14 15 16 17 18 19 1A 1B 1C 1D 1E 1F 20 21 22 23 24 25

Is this starting to seem logical yet?

There's just one more thing:

96 97 98 99 9A 9B 9C 9D 9E 9F A0 A1 A2 A3 A4

So A5 is bigger than 96. The hexadecimal numbers run out like this:

EA EB EC ED EE EF F0 F1 F2 F3 F4 F5 F6 F7 F8 F9 FA FB FC FD FE FF

38

FF is the number 254. The next number in the sequence would be 100, but FF is as high as the RGB colours go.

The best way to invent web colours manually is simply to experiment. If you want a reddish colour, use a high number for red and lower numbers for green and blue. Another useful tip is that the lower the numbers are overall, the darker the colour will be.

If you make a colour you like but want a lighter shade, just add on a number to each of the three values. To darken it, subtract in the same way. You can create a 'suite' of colours that go together in this way. We'll see some examples of this later in the chapter.

Fig. 15. The Windows Calculator is a standard accessory. It can be used to convert between decimal and hexadecimal numbers quickly and easily. Just type in the number and click Hex or Dec to convert.

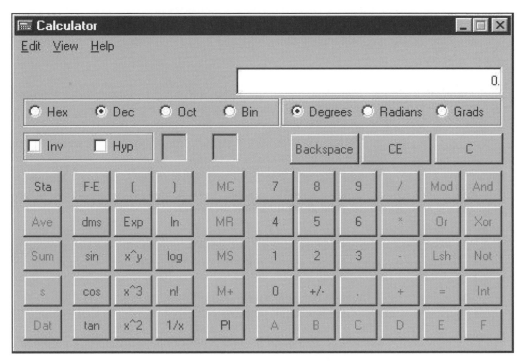

Setting a background colour

You already know how to specify the background colour by using the 'bgcolor' attribute of the <body> tag. You can set any colour you like as a background, but there are some practical considerations to keep in mind:

1. Your text is going to have to sit on top of it. Try to pick either a very light colour, or a very dark one. In this way black or white text will really stand out.

2. If you use a colour in which the red, green and blue values are quite similar, it will appear 'muted'. '#AABB99', for example, is a nice greenish brown which would work well behind black text.

3. If all the numbers you pick are the same, the result will be grey. This doesn't look too good on a web site unless you have some pretty special graphics.

Creating colours and graphics...

Setting text colours

To set your text in a different colour from the default black, use the 'color' attribute of the <font> tag:

```
<font color='#AE0062'>
```

Font colour is one of the things people often get wrong. Nobody, but nobody, wants to look at an orange screen with blue writing on it. Here are some things that do work:

(a) Light-coloured background with black text.
(b) Black background with white or very light-coloured text.
(c) Nearly black background (eg '#282F1E') with very light or white text.

And some more risky tactics...

▶ Use a light colour for background, and then a much darker shade of the same colour for text. For example, if the background colour is '#EE66FF' then set your text in something like '#9911AA'. (Remember that you can make a darker shade by reducing all the numbers by the same amount.)

▶ Create complementary colours just by switching red, blue and green values around. For example, if your background is '#EE66FF', try setting text in '#66FFEE' or '#FFEE66'.

The one place you might feel safe about using coloured text is in headings. Open up one of your brainstorming pages, give it a lightcoloured background, and only set the font colour for the heading, like this:

```
<body bgcolor='#D8EFFE'>
<font face='Arial, Helvetica'>
<p><font size='5' color='#AE0062'>Heading</font></p>
<p><font size='2' color='#000000'>Here is the text underneath
the heading. You'd probably want to type in a few extra lines to see the
full effect.</font></p>
</font>
</body>
```

Look at this example carefully if you're confused by how the tags are organised. I could have written it like this:

```
<body bgcolor='#D8EFFE'>
<font face='Arial, Helvetica'>
<p><font size='5'><font color='#AE0062'>Heading
</font></font></p>
<p><font size='2'><font color='#000000'>Here is the text
underneath the heading. You'd probably want to type in a few extra
lines to see the full effect.</font></font></p>
</font>
</body>
```

The effect is exactly the same, but it takes longer to type that way. I could also have used <font color='black'> instead of <font color='#000000'> if I was feeling really lazy.

▶ *Note 1* – The black text is given colour '#000000' (black). Actually, if you missed this out, most people's browsers would display it in black anyway because that's the default colour. The key word here is 'most'. It's worth putting it in for those few people using a browser with a different default text colour.

▶ *Note 2* – About one in three men are red/green colour-blind. This is another good reason not to mix background and foreground colours too murkily: you may find that many readers can't really see the text at all.

Creating graphics on the web

Colour is one of the basic elements of web page design, graphics are another. Most decent web sites do use graphics, and some awful ones do too. When you're thinking about design, always ask yourself: what does this graphic add to my page? Does it make it prettier, easier to use or more informative? If the answer is none of these, get rid of it.

That said, it's time to learn how to place graphics on your page and experiment with them. Don't worry about the look of the graphics to start with, just tinker.

Basic principles
Graphics on the web can have a number of different formats. The format of the graphic determines how the computer holds the information. Different formats are suitable for different things.

The most common format on your computer is probably the 'bitmap' format. To create a bitmap file, open up Paint or whatever your standard drawing package is called. Draw a few squiggles and save it. The filename should read something like 'squiggles.bmp'. The 'bmp' filename extension at the end tells your computer that it's a bitmap graphic file.

Although bitmaps are the easiest files to create, the disadvantage is that they're the biggest of all. When people are waiting for your page to appear, they don't want to have to wait for bitmaps, which are far bigger than other formats, however basic the image.

That's why the JPEG (pronounced 'jay-peg') and GIF formats were invented. They store graphical information much more economically. You'll find that most web graphics are GIFs, but JPEGs have their uses, too. We'll come to that shortly.

Downloading graphics

Before you can insert a graphic into a web page, you'll need a graphic to experiment with. One excellent source of web graphics is, of course, the internet itself. There are many places to get free graphics on the web, from funky designer pictures to everyday buttons, arrows and lines. Here are a couple (there are literally thousands out there):

Creating colours and graphics..

Transparent. For light backgrounds;
hand2.gif
Transparent. For dark backgrounds;
hand2D.gif

Transparent. For light backgrounds;
hand2R.gif
Transparent. For dark backgrounds;
hand2RD.gif

Transparent. For light backgrounds;
hand3.gif
Transparent. For dark backgrounds;
hand3D.gif

Transparent. For light
backgrounds;hand3R.gif
Transparent. For dark backgrounds;
hand3RD.gif

Fig. 16. Shawn's Clipart site is one of many sites run by aspiring (and often very good) graphic artists who make their work available over the internet for free.

http://www.gold.ac.uk/gifs/gifs4us/readme.htm

http://www.inforamp.net/~dredge/

Alternatively, you can also grab any graphic you like from any page on the internet using this simple technique (in 32-bit Windows systems):

1. Point the cursor at the graphic you want.

2. Click the right mouse button.

3. Select 'Save image as' or 'Save picture as'.

4. Choose the folder on your computer where you want to save your picture, and give it a name.

Bingo! There's the graphic file, right on your hard drive.

▶   *Important* – Never use someone else's graphic on a web site which you publish on the internet, without their written permission. People have been taken to court for doing this; it isn't worth it. Use these images for learning on your own PC, but don't get too attached to them because you can't usually keep them in the final version. Some web sites give permission to use their graphics, including, of course, sites which provide clip art and web graphics for that specific purpose.

If the graphic is moving while you point at it, it may well be something else. For now, leave it alone and choose something stationary instead. We'll talk a little about animating your graphics – getting them to move and change – later.

Creating your own graphics

You can use any graphics package you like to create images for your web site. Don't worry if you 'can't draw'. Be bold, and make simple shapes which work for the image of your site. Try scribbly, childlike ones or use a big brush to make blocky arrows, blobs and lines.

One very common type of image would be the name of your web site, written in a fancy font and decorated with colours or special effects. Have a look at the textures programs like which Microsoft Photo Editor and Adobe PhotoShop can apply to pictures. Here are some places to find interesting fonts for your logo graphic:

    http://www.allfreesites.com/fonts.html
    http://www.amazingresources.com/
    http://www.fontempire.com/
    http://www.fontfreak.com/index2.htm
    http://www.fontsnthings.com/
    http://research.umbc.edu/~mzhong1/font.html

Try typing the name of your site in a large, interesting font, adding colour and extra oddments, and using it as a heading at the top of your pages. You can also find 'dingbat' fonts on these sites, which contain little pictures instead of ordinary letters. These can come in very handy.

▶ *Note* – Why put this in a graphic if it's just your site's name in a fancy font? Remember, that fancy font probably won't be on your readers' computers, so if you wrote the name as text and set the font attribute, most people would just see it in their default font, missing the results of your efforts completely.

You may want to download a graphics package from the internet if you are not happy with the one that is already on your system. If so, try Paint

Fig. 17. The popular software program Paint Shop Pro can be used to create funky headings for your site, especially when combined with cool fonts like this one.

Shop Pro. It can be downloaded from JASC:

http://www.jasc.com/psp.html

Paint Shop Pro is quite a large program, so it will take a little while to download. Being more advanced than the average drawing package, it has rather a steep learning curve. The results you can get from it, however, are excellent.

If you want very slick images, and you're not a graphic designer, don't get frustrated. Just download them from somewhere. You can always open them in your graphics package and play around with them a bit if you want to add a personal touch. If you alter them enough – that is, beyond recognition – then you may be able to use them without crediting their original creator, but be very careful about doing this. Ask yourself whether the original creator could recognise their graphic as the source for yours. If they could, don't use it without permission.

▶ *Tip 1* – Be sure to pick colours that go well with your background colour, if you've already chosen one.

▶ *Tip 2* – Leave the actual background of your image white. If it's to be converted into a GIF, you can make this transparent later so that your background colour shows through.

Picking the right graphics format

Web site graphics *files* should be as small as possible. This is because the larger the file, the longer your visitors will have to wait before it appears on the page. That doesn't mean the *image* should be small. To check the file size, use Internet Explorer (in Windows 95/98), File Manager (in Windows 3.x) or a similar program. Make sure above all that your logo image, or any other image you are likely to use frequently, is a very small file. A simple GIF should compress down to around 2kb and will load very quickly. A graphic of 10kb or 20kb will really make an impact on the length of time your page takes to load up.

Most simple graphics packages will save your picture as a bitmap. In that case, you will need to use another package for turning your graphic into a GIF or JPEG. Microsoft Photo Editor, which comes as standard with Microsoft Office, can do this for you. Just open the file using this program, and choose 'Save as' If you don't have a program that can convert between different graphics file formats, try one of these freeware or shareware packages:

IrfanView
http://stud1.tuwien.ac.at/~e9227474/

2020s
http://www.mato.demon.nl/frw/graph.htm

BSGIFTA
http://www.geocities.com/SiliconValley/Peaks/6312/en_gifta.htm

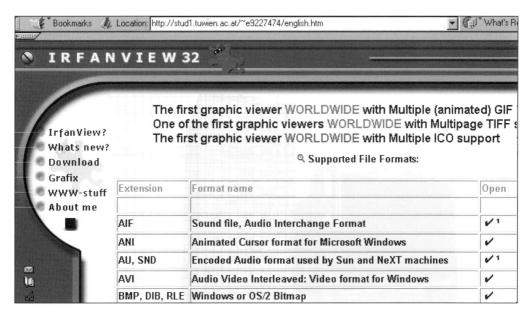

| Bookmarks | Location: | http://stud1.tuwien.ac.at/~e9227474/english.htm | What's R |

IRFANVIEW 32

IrfanView?
Whats new?
Download
Grafix
WWW-stuff
About me

The first graphic viewer WORLDWIDE with Multiple (animated) GIF
One of the first graphic viewers WORLDWIDE with Multipage TIFF
The first graphic viewer WORLDWIDE with Multiple ICO support

Supported File Formats:

Extension	Format name	Open
AIF	Sound file, Audio Interchange Format	✔¹
ANI	Animated Cursor format for Microsoft Windows	✔
AU, SND	Encoded Audio format used by Sun and NeXT machines	✔¹
AVI	Audio Video Interleaved: Video format for Windows	✔
BMP, DIB, RLE	Windows or OS/2 Bitmap	✔

Desktop98
http://desktop98.com/win98/graphic_tools.htm
This site has lots of graphics utilities for downloading.

Fig. 18. Irfanview is one of the many applications designed to convert bitmap files into smaller and quicker-loading GIF and JPEG file formats. Irfanview can be down-loaded free from the internet.

Use the GIF format if your image has clean lines and not too many colours. You'll see a lot of web graphics like this, and the reason is that they are very fast-loading. If you have simple images in GIF format, you can have lots of them and your page should still load pretty quickly.

GIF works by compressing horizontal lines of dots of the same colour. If you are designing images from scratch, remember this as you design them. Images with hundreds of colours, speckled patterns or airbrushed highlights aren't going to compress as well as flat, two- or three-colour ones.

If you want to make your image load faster and the colours are a bit fuzzy or complicated, you can use Photo Editor or many other graphics programs to 'posterise' it. This reduces the number of different colours in the picture and is well worth trying out. You can get a similar effect by reducing the 'colour depth' from, say, 32-bit to 8-bit, although the results are sometimes a bit too brutal. Experimentation is the key. Always save your work, and make a point of knowing how many actions your graphics package will allow you to Undo.

If your images aren't suited to this kind of treatment, you might want to use the JPEG format instead. JPEG uses a complicated system of compromises to make images smaller. It's ideal for photographs and other images which don't have the clean, sharp lines GIFs use. You can choose the level of compression. The greater the compression, the poorer the quality of the image. Reduce the quality until you think it's unacceptable. Then increase it gently to find the best compression level.

Creating colours and graphics...

Placing a graphic on your page

Before you put a graphic on your page, find the one you want to use. Make sure it is in the same directory (folder) as the web pages you've been experimenting with. This way, your browser will be able to find it.

Now, choose a page and open it up in both your browser and text editor. To insert an image, choose the position on the page that you would like to put it. Then type the 'image' tag, <img/>. The image tag doesn't need to be turned off (just like the <br /> tag). Let's say your image is called 'example.gif'. Here's how to insert the image:

```
< img src='example.gif'/>
```

The 'src' attribute tells it where the SouRCe of the image can be found – the file with the image in it.

Example
Here's an example of a page with a few graphics (Figure 19). For this, you'll need an image called 'heading.gif' which is a fairly large logo, and one called 'button.gif' which is a small button. Of course, the buttons won't do anything yet. We will come to that later.

```
<html>
<head>
<title>The World of the Pre-Raphaelites: Index</title>
</head>
<body>
<font face='Arial, Helvetica' size='3'>
<p align='center'> <img src='heading.gif'/> </p>
<p>Here is an index of what's on this web site: </p>
<p> <img src='button.gif'/> Introduction to the
   Pre-Raphaelites<br />
<img src='button.gif'/> Painting and sculpture<br />
<img src='button.gif'/> Literature<br />
<img src='button.gif'/> Philosophy<br />
<img src='button.gif'/> Links to other Pre-Raphaelite sites on
   the web<br /> </p>
</font>
</body>
</html>
```

Notice that the centred heading image is in a paragraph on its own. Also, notice how the button graphics appear at the start of each line, pretty much as you would expect. Try moving <img/> tags around and you will soon get a feel for how they work.

Controlling image size

For this one, you'll need 'button.gif' to be very small if the page is to look any good. It certainly shouldn't be larger than 20 pixels square. If you

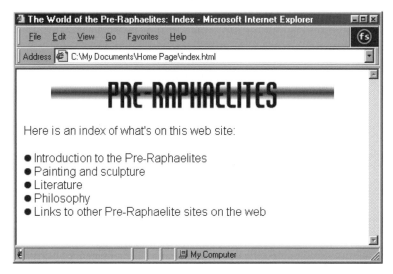

The World of the Pre-Raphaelites: Index - Microsoft Internet Explorer

File   Edit   View   Go   Favorites   Help

Address C:\My Documents\Home Page\index.html

PRE-RAPHAELITES

Here is an index of what's on this web site:

● Introduction to the Pre-Raphaelites
● Painting and sculpture
● Literature
● Philosophy
● Links to other Pre-Raphaelite sites on the web

My Computer

Fig. 19. Here is a page which uses an image as its heading. You might not think that this style is very suitable for the subject matter, though.

have an image you want to use again and again at different sizes, you can do it like this:

< img src='button.gif' height='10' width='10'/ >

If button.gif is 20 pixels high and 20 wide, this tag will display it at half that size – which is pretty tiny. If your buttons were a bit on the big side, try setting the height and width in this way.

Obviously, you should only do this if you want to use the full-sized image somewhere else. Otherwise, make a new image that is exactly the size you want. It's hard to draw very tiny images, so consider using a bigger image size, doodling until you get something you like, and then copying it over into a new image that *is* the right size. Alternatively, you can use most graphics packages to shrink an image to the size you want.

If you can use the same graphic in different sizes, your site will load much faster than one which uses several different graphics, because each separate graphic on your site has to travel down your reader's telephone line, at which point it's temporarily stored on the computer. If the browser sees a different graphic, it has to pull that one down the phone line as well, causing a delay. If the graphic has been used recently, it will just pick it up off the local hard drive, which is much faster.

Transparency

You may want to have a graphic that sits neatly on top of your coloured background. It will look as if your picture has been carefully cut out and pasted onto the page. If you drew your own images, hopefully you took my advice and left the background white; this will help a lot.

The easiest way to do this with a GIF is by using transparency. Any program which lets you edit pictures and save them as GIFs will enable you to choose a colour and set it as the 'background' or 'transparent' colour. That way you won't get an unwanted white rectangle around your nice logo. Instead the logo will sit very professionally on your page.

The technique for setting transparency differs for different graphics

47

programs, but it is usually very simple. Check the help file for details. Unless you have a good reason, all your images should have a transparent background if they're not images of rectangular things.

Using a graphic as a background

It's easy and fun to give your web page a picture as its background instead of using a flat colour. You use the < body > tag again, this time setting the 'background' attribute:

< body background='button.gif' >

Fig. 20. Using an image as a background to your web page isn't difficult, but that doesn't mean it's always a good idea.

Try this; the chances are that the results will be horrible. Your browser interprets this instruction as meaning 'repeat the graphic over and over, all over the background of the document'. This is called 'tiling'. It does not usually produce a very attractive result. Here are some hints for making graphical backgrounds work successfully:

1. Use an image which is either very dark or very light, with not too much that's distracting.

2. Generally speaking, the larger the background image, the worse the effect.

3. Try an image one pixel high or one pixel wide, in one colour with a single dot in another colour. These will give you stripes running horizontally or vertically, respectively.

4. Always, always specify a 'bgcolor' for the page that matches the colour of the tiled image. Some people browse the web with their graphics turned off. Don't upset them by presenting them with white text on a white background just because your image is very dark.

5. There are a few programs that will create tiling images for you. One such is Sausage software's Reptile. It's fascinating to play with and watch as it uses mathematical algorithms to generate natural-looking patterns.

    http://www.sausage.com/reptile/reptile.html

6. Background images are another thing which beginners get hideously wrong. Take a look at some sites that do this and you may be put off the whole thing for a while. Few professional web sites have background images, and even fewer have good ones.

Finally, here's a little thing you might enjoy:

```
< body background='button.gif' bgproperties='fixed' >
```

The only way to experience this one is to try it on a page full of text. It keeps the background still while you scroll down, but it only works in Internet Explorer at the time of writing, so a number of your audience won't see the effect. Still, you might want to put it into your pages if they have enough text to force the reader to scroll down past the bottom of the screen. It won't crash non-Explorer browsers, which will just ignore it completely.

Degradable design: the 'alt' parameter

Soon, we'll see how to make your graphics do things. If you have graphics which do things, or which are important in any other way, remember that some people have very slow connections and choose to 'surf' with graphics turned off. Instead of a graphic on your page, they will see an empty box; instead of your background image (if you have one) they'll see the 'bgcolor'.

Help these people by using the 'alt' attribute of the image tag. It tells the browser what to display if, for any reason, it can't display the image:

```
< img src='button.gif' alt='Button' / >
```

Not only will this say 'Button' if, for some reason, it can't see the graphic, but in most browsers it will say 'Button' if someone points at it but isn't sure whether or not to click it. That's very useful.

There are two schools of thought on this: you could make the 'alt' text describe the graphic ('Button'), or you could make it describe what the button does ('Click here to go to'). That's up to you, but as a recommendation:

1. If your site has a lot of graphics, make your 'alt' attributes very clear so that someone could use the site without the images themselves.

2. If it just has a few buttons and other things, assume your audience can see the images. Your 'alt' texts will still help blind users, visitors with extremely slow connections and those using some emerging methods of web access.

4 Creating links and tables

In this chapter we will explore:

► *creating links between pages*
► *text links*
► *graphical links*
► *using tables to layout your text and graphics*
► *table alignment and spanning*
► *colours and graphics in tables*

. . . .

Creating links between pages

Links are what make web pages web pages. They're the 'hyper' in 'hypertext', which is why they're often called 'hyperlinks'. In a book, each page follows on from the other. In a web site, the pages are linked together in a sort of network, and different readers can follow the links in whatever sequence they wish.

Mastering links is essential for setting up a web site. Fortunately, it's pretty easy. For the material in this section, you will need a handful of web pages (at the very least, two) in your web page directory. Hopefully you have these already. If not, quickly create two or three dummy pages.

At this stage don't worry too much about which pages should be linked together and how to present your site to readers. Here, we are simply learning the technicalities. In the next chapter, we'll take a look at how to organise a web site and prepare it for publication.

Text links

The simplest – and often the best – kind of link is the text link. Go to almost any web site and you'll see bits of text which are formatted differently from the others. They are probably underlined and might well be blue. You already know what these are: text links. If you put your cursor on top of one, it turns into a pointing finger, indicating that if you click on the text you will go to another page.

To create this effect, you use the <a> tag. The 'a' stands for 'anchor'. The anchor tag can do a number of things, but in this case we want it to create a hyperlink. We give it the page's filename in the 'href' (Hyperlink REFerence) attribute. On page1.html you might have a link like this:

```
<a href='page2.html'>Go to page two</a>
```

Try this and view it in the browser. Instantly, you have blue underlined text. Point at it, and you have a pointing finger. Click it, and page2.html appears. Simple!

Controlling how text links look
If your background is blue, or if you don't like blue, this blue underlined

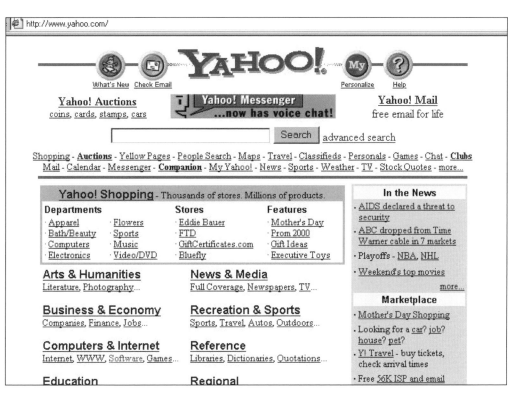

link will doubtless not be to your liking. Fortunately, you can set the colours of hyperlinks using more attributes of the <body> tag:

```
<body link='#008000' vlink='#808000' alink='#FF00FF'>
```

The 'link' attribute sets the colour for ordinary links. You might have noticed that links tend to change colour after you've visited them; well, you can tell the browser to use a different colour for these with the 'vlink' (Visited LINK) attribute. Of course, you can choose any colours you like.

The 'alink' attribute tells it what colour to use for links which are currently active. You won't see this very often, but if a new page takes a little while to load up then it will turn this colour while the page is opening. You may as well set this while you're at it.

If you don't like the underlining, you can get rid of it using the 'style' attribute of the <a> tag, like this:

```
<p> <a href='page2.html' style='text-decoration: none'> Go to
page two </a> </p>
```

Unfortunately, you have to set this for each link individually, but it's worth it if that is really the look you want. Remember that the setting up of web pages usually involves using templates and lots of cutting and pasting, so don't worry about having to type all this in too many times.

There are a lot more styles you can set, but since this is the only one

Fig. 21. Like most web sites, Yahoo! has an index page which contains dozens of links to the content inside. Each link is clearly underlined and coloured blue by the browser to show the user that it is a link waiting to be clicked.

that can get rid of the underline, it's the only one of much use to us here. Try 'text-decoration: line-through' or 'text-decoration: overline' and you'll see how pointless these things really are. The other styles are obtainable in other ways, for example using the <b> tag for bold.

Removing underlining and giving your links custom colours can really give your page some identity. Keep in mind that people do need some clues to what is a hyperlink and what is not, so make sure there's something distinctive about them. If you're not sure they're distinctive enough, you could try typing the link text in CAPITALS.

▶ *Note* – The 'style' attribute comes from the world of 'cascading style sheets'. Not all browsers support style sheets. Those that don't will ignore the 'style' attribute and give your link an underline anyway.

Graphical links

You can turn a graphic – such as a button – into a link by using the <a> tag in exactly the same way. Here's an example:

```
<a  href='page2.html'> <img src='button.gif' /> </a>  Painting
and sculpture <br>
```

Now, at last, our button does something. Look at it in the browser, though, and you'll see an unsightly blue border around the edge. (It will be a link-coloured border, if you've changed the colours of your links on this page.) That's easy to get rid of, this time using the 'border' attribute of the <a> tag:

```
<a href='page2.html' border='0'>
```

There – much better! You need only leave the border in place if it's not at all obvious that the graphic might work as a link.

If you are using graphics as links, try to make it obvious what they do. That sounds self-evident, but it's amazing how many designer sites are

Fig. 22. Images used as links normally have a blue border around them, to announce the fact. You can remove this by using the 'border' attribute of the <a /> tag.

covered in incomprehensible navigation images. If you frustrate your readers, most of them will quickly leave.

Which graphics to use?
This isn't something to worry too much about right now, but bear in mind that your graphics may not appear in every single reader's browser. It's always safest to provide text links somewhere on the page to help those people.

Nevertheless, graphical links are definitely part of the language of the web. My advice? Offer both options to your visitors. Those who can see the graphics will hardly notice the text links. Those who cannot will be glad the links are there.

You might like to experiment with having a row of small text links at the top or bottom of each page, enabling the reader to jump to any page on your site without getting in the way. There's a trick to getting this to look right; here's an example:

```
< p align='center' >
< a href='index.htm' > Main page < /a >
& nbsp;        
< a href='cv.htm' > Curriculum Vitae < /a >
         
< a href='goal.htm' > Career goals < /a >
< /p >
```

The code ' '
You might be rather puzzled by the code ' '. Don't be. This is HTML's weird way of telling your browser you want a space there. Browsers recognise a single space quite happily, but if you want a row of spaces then you need a special kind of space called a non-breaking space.   inserts one for you. You'll find that this bit of code is very handy for pushing text around into the places you want, as we did in this example.

▶ *Note* – There are lots of characters which HTML can display using this notation. For example, most newer browsers understand *€*. This might be useful if you are creating a financial site. You can find a list of most of these codes here:

http://htmlgoodies.earthweb.com/&command.html

Using tables to lay out your text and graphics

Tables are one of the toughest things to master in HTML. What they offer, though, is well worth the effort. If the rest of this chapter starts to feel a bit daunting, ignore it for now and move onto the next. You can always come back and explore tables later. Tables aren't necessary for setting up your first web site, but they are used so widely now and are so handy that you will probably want to get your teeth into them sooner or later.

Creating links and tables ···

Getting more control

Tables give you a way to control how your text and graphics appear on the page. Perhaps you have used tables in a word processor to make professional-looking layouts. For example, you may have created a main body of text with other text or graphics running down the side.

Tables work by creating a grid of invisible 'boxes' on your page. These boxes ('cells') can be positioned however you like, within reason. In each box you can put whatever HTML you want: text, graphics, links or any combination of these.

Most really professional-looking web sites use tables extensively. Here we'll learn how to make simple ones, and how to make simple ones more complex.

The principles of tables

HTML tables are notoriously strange. You'll have to take my word for much of what follows. It works, but the reasons why it works are a bit obscure. The best way to learn how to set up a table is to look at a simple example, like this one:

```
<table border='2' width='100%' height='100%'>
  <tr>
    <td width='50%' height='50%'>X</td>
    <td width='50%' height='50%'>X</td>
  </tr>
  <tr>
    <td width='50%' height='50%'>X</td>
    <td width='50%' height='50%'>X</td>
  </tr>
</table>
```

Fig. 23. A web page designed by the author. It illustrates the use of tables to create layouts by using columns, headings and other effects.

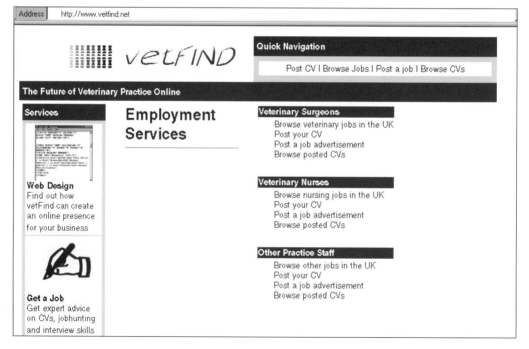

Address http://www.vetfind.net

vetFIND

Quick Navigation

Post CV I Browse Jobs I Post a job I Browse CVs

The Future of Veterinary Practice Online

Services

Web Design
Find out how vetFind can create an online presence for your business

Get a Job
Get expert advice on CVs, jobhunting and interview skills

Employment Services

Veterinary Surgeons
Browse veterinary jobs in the UK
Post your CV
Post a job advertisement
Browse posted CVs

Veterinary Nurses
Browse nursing jobs in the UK
Post your CV
Post a job advertisement
Browse posted CVs

Other Practice Staff
Browse other jobs in the UK
Post your CV
Post a job advertisement
Browse posted CVs

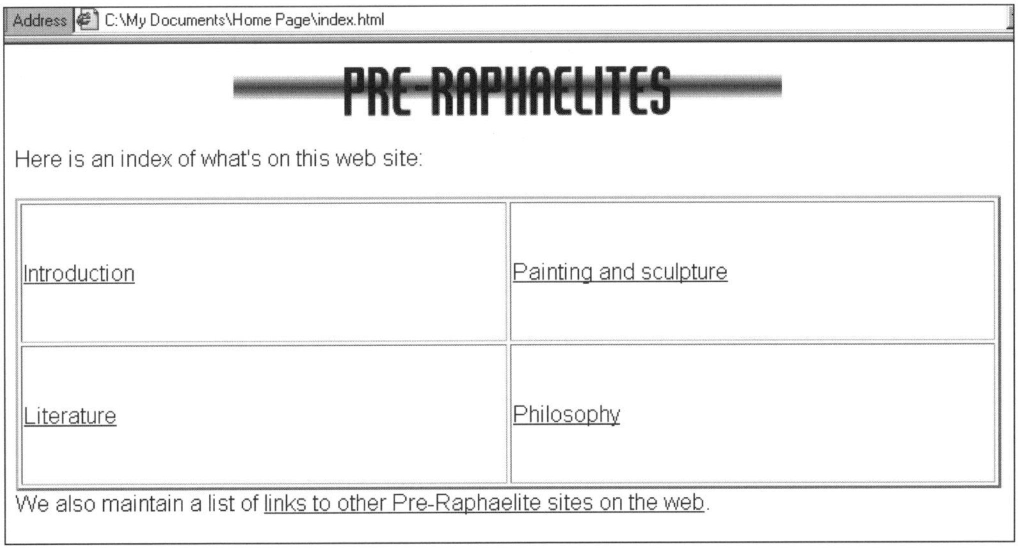

Address C:\My Documents\Home Page\index.html

PRE-RAPHAELITES

Here is an index of what's on this web site:

Introduction	Painting and sculpture
Literature	Philosophy

We also maintain a list of links to other Pre-Raphaelite sites on the web.

That's a simple example. The very first step is to type this carefully into an HTML page, and then view it in your browser. You will then see a table with two rows and two columns – four spaces, each of which currently has a letter 'X' in it. Type anything you want instead of 'X'. It's just there in this example so that your browser has something to display.

▶ *Note* – You don't have to 'indent' the different lines of code. It is just done to make it as clear as possible. You could put the whole thing on a single line of text if you really wanted to.

Now, let's break this down and see how it works. We start with the <table> tag:

```
<table border='2' width='100%' height='100%'>

...

</table>
```

This tells your browser that what's between these two tags will be some kind of table. It tells it how wide and high the whole table should be in relation to the available space in the browser's window. It also gives it a border, so that you can see it. When you've finished designing a table, you can set the 'border' attribute to '0' to make the table invisible.

▶ *Tip* – You can also specify widths and heights in pixels. The problem with this is that different people, with their various high- or low-resolution screens, will see different results. It's safest to use percentages unless you know that your table cells must be a particular pixel size (for example, if you are using them to precisely lay out graphic images).

Fig. 24. A simple example of a table. Amazingly, this contains all the code you need to create most of the great layouts you see on professional sites.

55

Creating links and tables ....

Here's the next tag to look at: `<tr>` `</tr>`. It stands for 'Table Row'. You define HTML tables a row at a time. That's just how you do it – each row is defined separately.

Within each row, you'll want a number of spaces or 'cells'. Each of these is defined by the `<td>` tag, which describes what Table Data is in each row, and how it's divided up. This is one of the most confusing things about HTML tables, but there it is. You warn the browser that a row is about to start, then describe each cell which is in the row, one at a time.

Each separate set of Table Data – that is, each cell – needs its width and height specifying. Make sure that the widths of the cells in each `<tr>` adds up to the width of the table (which you specified in the `<table>` tag). Also, make sure that the height of each `<td>` in any one row is the same. The heights of the `<td>`s in the `<tr>`s must add up to the height of the table as a whole. If this gives you a headache, just look at the numbers in the example and it should be clearer.

Some examples to make things clearer
Imagine you wanted an extra row in this example table. Here's how the code might look:

```
<table border='2' width='100%' height='100%'>
  <tr>
    <td width='50%' height='30%'>X</td>
    <td width='50%' height='30%'>X</td>
  </tr>
  <tr>
    <td width='50%' height='30%'>X</td>
    <td width='50%' height='30%'>X</td>
  </tr>
  <tr>
    <td width='50%' height='40%'>THIS IS OUR NEW ROW</td>
    <td width='50%' height='40%'>AND SO IS THIS!</td>
  </tr>
</table>
```

We've simply added an extra `<tr>` section at the bottom of the table. Notice also, though, that we have reduced the heights of the `<td>`s to fit them into our '100%' space. Because 30 + 30 + 40 = 100%, this is correct. Try it yourself, and try some other variations, too.

▶ *Note* – Browsers are rather flaky about tables with a height of over 100%. Trial and error is the best way to persuade them to display what you intended. Alternatively, you can use multiple tables. For example:

```
<table border='2' width='100%' height='100%'>
  <tr>
    <td width='50%' height='50%'>X</td>
    <td width='50%' height='50%'>X</td>
```

Address 🥑 C:\My Documents\Home Page\index.html

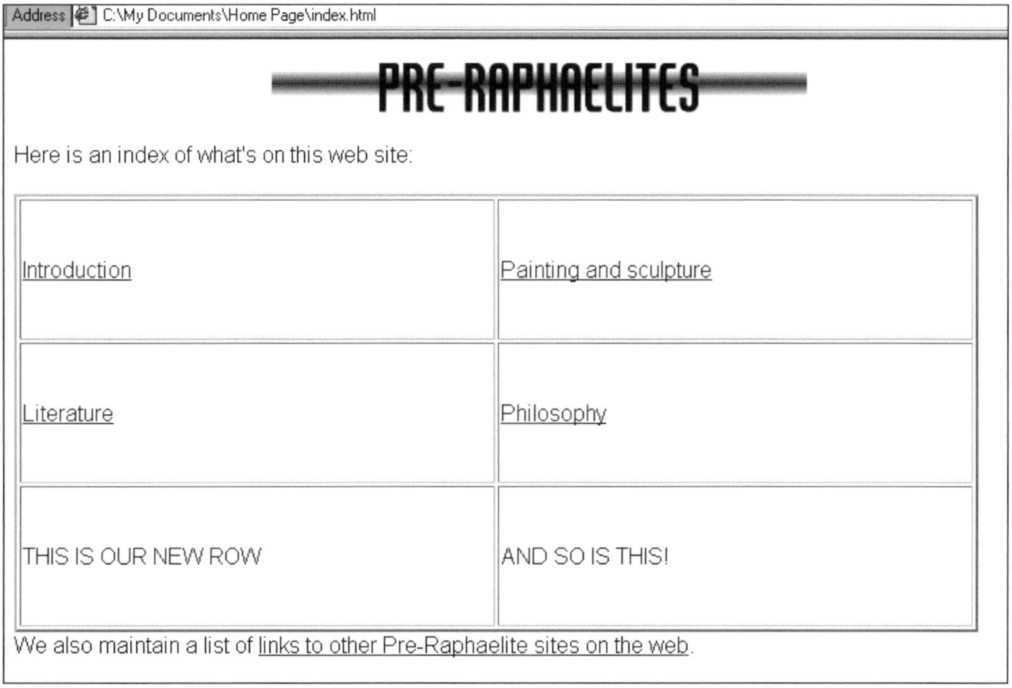

PRE-RAPHAELITES

Here is an index of what's on this web site:

Introduction	Painting and sculpture
Literature	Philosophy
THIS IS OUR NEW ROW	AND SO IS THIS!

We also maintain a list of links to other Pre-Raphaelite sites on the web.

```
    </tr>
    <tr>
        <td width='50%' height='50%'>X</td>
        <td width='50%' height='50%'>X</td>
    </tr>
</table>
<table border='2' width='100%' height='100%'>
    <tr>
        <td width='50%' height='50%'>X</td>
        <td width='50%' height='50%'>X</td>
    </tr>
    <tr>
        <td width='50%' height='50%'>X</td>
        <td width='50%' height='50%'>X</td>
    </tr>
</table>
```

Fig. 25. Adding an extra row to a table is pretty straightforward.

This works much better than a single table with a height of 200%, although you do get a small gap between the two tables, even when the border is set to 0. This might be a problem for you, depending on what you are doing.

Adding an extra column

How about adding an extra column? That's easy, too. For each table row, we need to add an extra piece of table data. If we wanted a large central column and narrower outer ones, it might look like this:

```
<table border='2' width='100%' height='100%'>
  <tr>
    <td width='20%' height='50%'>X</td>
    <td width='60%' height='50%'>X</td>
    <td width='20%' height='50%'>X</td>
  </tr>
  <tr>
    <td width='20%' height='50%'>X</td>
    <td width='60%' height='50%'>X</td>
    <td width='20%' height='50%'>X</td>
  </tr>
</table>
```

Try viewing this in your browser to see it in action. Experiment with adding rows and columns to tables before you move on.

When you're happy with a table layout, type in some text for each cell and set the 'border' attribute of the <table> tag to '0'. The borders will vanish, leaving you with the text exactly where you wanted it.

Table alignment and spanning

Better table layouts using alignment
You may have noticed that your text always sits inside the <td> cell like this:

1. Flush with the left-hand side of the <td> cell.

2. In the vertical centre of the cell – that is, not at the top or bottom, but in the middle.

You can get your text to align differently both vertically and horizontally. To change the horizontal alignment of your text, use the 'align' attribute of the <td> tag:

Fig. 26. You can also add a new column to a table, like this. 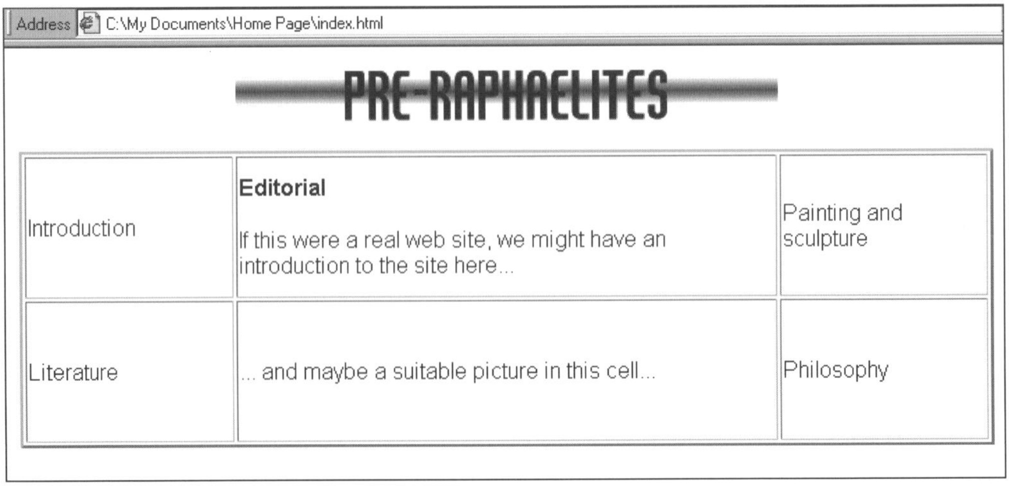

```
<td width='150%' height='50%' align='center'>X</td>
```

| Address | C:\My Documents\Home Page\index.html |

PRE-RAPHAELITES

| Introduction | **Editorial**

If this were a real web site, we might have an introduction to the site here... | Painting and sculpture |
| Literature | ... and maybe a suitable picture in this cell... | Philosophy |

You could also have used align='right' or (the default) align='left'. Here's a different way to do it:

```
<td width='150%' height='50%'> <p align='center'>X</p>
</td>
```

Remember, you can use any HTML you want in a table cell, and the <p> tag is no exception.

To get your text to sit at the top or bottom of your table, though, you do need to use an attribute of the <td> tag, 'valign' (Vertical ALIGN):

```
<td width='150' height='50%' valign='top'>X</td>
```

You could also use valign='bottom'. When you're developing real tables to put text into, being able to control the alignment from the <td> tag is extremely useful.

Better table layouts using spanning
Now it's time to learn a couple of tricks you can use to create more flexible tables. Be warned, though: you'll need to be sure you understand how the <tr> and <td> tags work to get the hang of these techniques.

Let's take our three-row, two-column table and imagine that we want the middle row to have just one cell which spans all three columns. That's a common enough situation and here's how it's done:

```
<table border='2' width='100%' height='300%'>
  <tr>
    <td width='50%' height='50%'>X</td>
    <td width='50%' height='50%'>X</td>
  </tr>
  <tr>
    <td width='100%' height='50%' colspan='2'>X</td>
  </tr>
  <tr>
    <td width='50%' height='50%'>X</td>
    <td width='50%' height='50%'>X</td>
  </tr>
</table>
```

Look at the middle row: we've put only one <td> in there, and made it as wide as the whole table. We've also set a new attribute, 'colspan', to '2'. 'Colspan' explains to your browser that you haven't made a mistake; you really did intend to make this cell two columns wide.

Easy? Well, it's not too bad. But how about making a cell that spans several rows? Think of a page which has a long index running down one side, and a main section with text and graphics sitting in several rows; it can be done. Here's our two-by-two table, with the first column covering two rows:

```
<table border='2' width='100%' height='100%'>
  <tr>
    <td width='50%' height='100%' rowspan='2'>X</td>
    <td width='50%' height='50%'>X</td>
  </tr>
  <tr>
    <td width='50%' height='50%'>X</td>
  </tr>
</table>
```

The first <td> is as high as the whole table, and this time we've used the 'rowspan' attribute to explain to the browser exactly what we want. Notice that in the second <tr> there's only one <td>. The browser will understand that you wanted the first column to be taken up by the cell you defined already, the one that spans two rows.

Row and column spanning is pretty hard to do, especially when you start combining spanned rows and spanned columns. It's very useful to draw out your layout on a piece of paper. Make sure you understand how it's going to work in terms of the grid of rows and columns which your browser is looking for. Then look at which cells need to span several rows and columns, and you should be well on your way to setting it up.

A note on font control in tables
It's an oddity of tables that you need to specify the <font> attributes for each <td>. This is where you might well want to use several attributes in the same tag, and just copy them into each <td> once the table is ready:

```
<table border='2' width='100%' height='100%'>
  <tr>
    <td width='50%' height='50%'> <font face='Arial, Helvetica'
      size='3'>X</font> </td>
    <td width='50%' height='50%'> <font face='Arial, Helvetica'
      size='3'>X</font> </td>
  </tr>
  <tr>
    <td width='50%' height='50%'> <font face='Arial, Helvetica'
      size='3'>X</font> </td>
    <td width='50%' height='50%'> <font face='Arial, Helvetica'
      size='3'>X</font> </td>
  </tr>
</table>
```

It's irritating, but it's the only thing most browsers will understand. Again, remember that you are likely to use the same table structure again and again on your real web pages, so you won't have to type all of this in every time.

▶ *Tip* – Cascading Style Sheets (CSS) are a recently-introduced extension to HTML that you will have seen mentioned a few times already in this book. They offer a way out of this madness. In time, it will be practical to remove all your font tags and just set a style for the whole table. Currently, though, this will result in nasty default behaviour from the numerous browsers that don't understand style sheets. By the time you read this, things may well have moved on.

Colours and graphics in tables

There are several nice visual things you can do with tables once you know how to set them up. When testing these out, remember to set the 'border' attribute of the <table> tag to '0' so that the lines disappear and the work which has gone into your layout becomes invisible.

Colouring in a cell
The easiest thing to do is make a cell coloured. You do this using the 'bgcolor' attribute of the <td> tag:

```
<td width='50%' height='50%' bgcolor='#AADDEE'>X</td>
```

This is a very quick and neat way to set off text which you want to draw attention to, making it clear that the text in this cell stands on its own.
    You can also use a graphic as a background, just as you can with your <body> tag:

```
<td width='50%' height='50%' background='texture.gif'>X</td>
```

As with the <body> tag, this will 'tile' your image all over the cell. If the image is too big, you will only see a part of it. It works well with a texture, but badly with most logos.

▶ *Tip* – You can make an image show once only as the background –
    for example, a very light-coloured logo which will sit behind your text.
    Use as the cell's background a graphic containing this image, plus a
    fairly large amount of empty space (which should be transparent). If
    the table cell is about the right size, it will work. If the file is a GIF, the
    increase in downloading speed will be negligible. Some 'tweaking' of
    cell size is usually necessary. Be sure to test it in both Explorer and
    Navigator, as results can vary.

Alternatively, you can place an image in the cell just as you'd place one anywhere else, using the <img/> tag:

```
<td width='50%' height='50%'>
  <p>Here's my logo:<br>
  <img src='logo.gif'/> <br>
  What do you think?</p>
</td>
```

This is broken up into separate lines to make it clearer, but you don't have to do this.

5 Putting your site together

In this chapter we will explore:

▶ *creating a logical plan for your whole site*
▶ *your imaginary visitor*
▶ *web site structures*
▶ *setting up a template page*
▶ *the index page*
▶ *using bookmarks*
▶ *the essential email link*
▶ *testing your site*

. . . .

Creating a logical plan for your whole site

The first step is to look at your content again and decide how many separate web pages you want to create. A good way to do this is to start by printing out all of your content. Then, try to organise it visually before you return to the computer screen.

Too much or too little content on a web page can be equally annoying. Between one and two full screens is about right, but if your content requires something different then do something different. There aren't any rules.

Make sure each page has a very clear theme and sticks to one type of content. Don't worry about visual design yet. Just make sure your content is dispersed over the number of pages you intend to create.

Also, don't be concerned if you have quite a lot of pages. We will see shortly how to create a design template, and how to copy your content into it for each page, so that creating twenty pages is hardly more time-consuming than creating five.

Your imaginary visitor

The next thing to consider is how you are going to present your pages to your reader. Imagine someone visiting your site for the first time. Will they find it confusing or clear? Will it grab their attention right away? If they're looking for specific information, will they be able to tell if it's there and reach it quickly?

Remember that many people aren't looking for extremely slick-looking sites with dancing pixies and sounds and games to play. Most people are just looking for useful content – the text matter which is at the heart of your site.

Don't be discouraged if your graphics skills aren't too strong, or your text is sitting on the page in a lump because you haven't yet mastered tables. Your audience probably won't care too much about these things. Their main concern is to find out what you have to tell them. As long as your site is clear and easy to read, they will probably stay.

Web site structures

The next thing to decide is how to link your pages together so that your imaginary visitor will find it easy to navigate around your site. There are two basic ways to structure a web site: hierarchically and non-hierarchically.

A hierarchical structure

A hierarchical site is shaped rather like a tree. The pages branch off one another to create increasingly detailed levels of information. An example is shown in figure 27. This strategy provides a structure which is simple to understand, especially if your content readily falls into distinct categories. Hierarchical sites are by far the most common on the web.

The downside is that hierarchical sites force visitors to follow certain pre-set paths. That's good if you think all your visitors will want to follow those paths, and if you make sure they will understand which path to follow. It also means that a user may have to go through several pages to find the information they are looking for. On a hierarchical web site, clear signposting is essential.

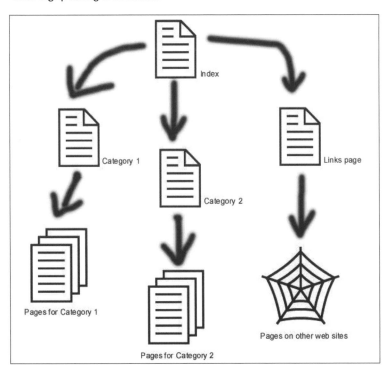

Fig. 27. A tree-like structure is easy to understand, but if your site has a lot of content your visitors may have to pass through several pages to arrive at the information they want.

A non-hierarchical structure

The alternative is to structure your site in a looser way, with connections crossing your categories. This is a good way to organise smaller sites with fewer pages, as in figure 28. This kind of structure encourages the visitor to jump from screen to screen until the right information comes up. If you have dozens and dozens of pages, a hierarchical structure might be

Putting your site together ....

Fig. 28. A looser, more web-like structure can be confusing to visitors, but if it's well-signposted and your content suits it then access to specific information can be quicker

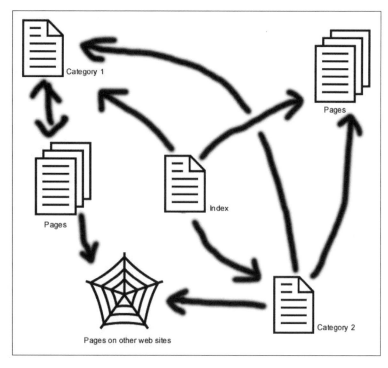

better, but smaller sites benefit from the extra accessibility the non-hierarchical structure brings.

Note that both kinds of structure have an 'index page'. This is essential. There is more about index pages below.

Setting up a template page

Once you've worked out how many pages you will have, and what will be on each one, it's time to start creating the pages themselves. It's strongly advised – particularly if you have more than three or four pages – that you start by creating a template page.

This will be a blank page which contains all of the standard stuff which you want to appear on every page, or most pages, in your site.

Essential components of a template
Here are some things you should include on your template page:

1. Of course, you'll need to start with the $<html>$, $<head>$ and $<body>$ tags, with their closing tags in the right places.

2. A $<title>$ is useful. If your web site is called 'I Love Jerry Springer' then make that the title, and then for each page you can add to it: 'I Love Jerry Springer: Biography', 'I Love Jerry Springer: Pictures' and so on. That gives your pages a coherent sense of identity.

3. Set the background colour and text and link colours using the $<body>$ tag. You can then forget about them.

Optional components of a template
Here are some things you might want to include, depending on the sort of layout you are using:

(a) A graphical logo for your site.

(b) An email link (explained below).

(c) Links to the main pages of your site, for example on a single line or in a column.

(d) A table framework. If you use tables on your site a lot, try to use the same table on many different pages. This will obviously save you a lot of grief.

(e) If you have decided on a hosting service (see the next chapter) there may be some HTML which you need to include on every page in order to support their advertising. This would go in the template too.

Create your template page just like any other web page. Then when you want to paste some content into it, save it with a new filename ('Save As') before you do.

The index page

Whenever someone types in your web site address, they will always see one particular page first. This is called the front page, or index page. As the second word implies, one of the best things you can do with an index page is to present the reader with a table of contents describing what is to be found on the site. You might want to make the index page the first one you design.

Essentials of the index page
Your index page *must*:

1. identify your site, giving the name of the site and a graphical logo if you have one,

2. explain what your site is about and what kinds of information can be found there,

3. contain a link to at least one other page.

In addition, it *should*:

(a) give hints about the structure of the site,

(b) include links to all of the main pages in the site,

(c) tempt the reader to stay with the site.

An index page should also be brief, to the point, and quick-loading. Don't overload it with flashy graphics or screens of text. If you want to have an

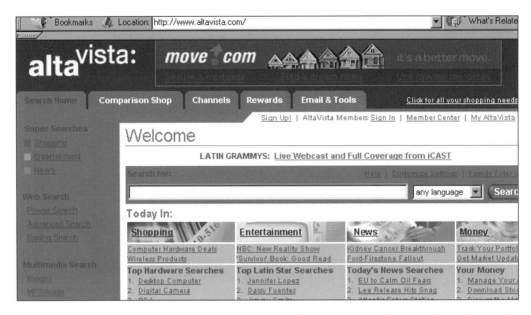

Fig. 29. A page with masses of content, which falls naturally into sections, benefits from a table of contents at the top. This helps the reader to navigate through what might otherwise appear to be a confusing mass of information.

'editorial'-style article describing your personal reasons for setting up the site or including what's there, then consider hiving this off onto a separate page called About, or something similar.

If you can, try to cram the whole index page contents into one screen. It will look much more professional that way. You could try setting your index page in a table, with links to the rest of the site in one cell and information about the site in another. The 'links' cell could be narrower than the 'about' cell, so that the links appear to be set in a slim column running down the side of the text. This style may or may not work for your site, but there are many sites which do use it, so it will already be familiar to your readers.

Remember that your experience, in common with most other people's, is probably that most web sites are not what you're looking for. When searching for something on the web, it's very common to visit only the first page of a site, evaluate it, and then quickly move on if it's obviously not what you want. There are simply too many sites out there – over a billion – for us to check through every one we come across. Make very sure that your index page is one that will encourage readers to stop and explore further.

Using bookmarks

You may have a page that contains large amounts of text, taking up more than two screens. If so, you could use bookmarks to create a table of contents for that page. To do this, split up your page into sub-headings. Next, 'bookmark' each sub-heading using the 'name' attribute of the < a > tag, like this:

    < p > < a name='intro' > < /a > Introduction. < /p >

Notice that the < /a > tag appears immediately after the < a > tag. That's unusual, but it is part of this trick. Basically, these two tags together identify this point as the 'intro'.

Now, let's say we have created several sub-headings like this one for a page about choosing flowers for your outdoor planters. We've named them Intro, Colours, Season, Size and Conclusion. We could put something like this at the start of the page:

```
<p>The following article explains some of the things to consider
when planning an outdoor display. It contains the following sections:
<blockquote>
<a href='#intro'>Introduction</a><br>
<a href='#colours'>Choosing your colours</a><br>
<a href='#season'>Balancing flowering seasons</a><br>
<a href='#size'>Height and spread of your plants</a><br>
<a href='#conclusion'>Putting it all together</a>
</blockquote></p>
```

The thing to notice here is what goes in the 'href' attribute. It is the name of the bookmark, preceded by a '#' which tells your browser that this is a bookmark on the current page.

Finally, you could bookmark the very top of the page, where the heading is, enabling your readers to jump back to this from each paragraph, like this:

```
… Of course, there are many other questions you should ask yourself
as you prepare your display, but answering the questions of colour,
season and size will give you an excellent place to start.<br>
<a href='#top'>TOP</a></p>
```

It's not essential to do this, but now you know how to do it should you want to.

Fig. 30. An example of the use of bookmarks to create a table of contents on a web page. The bookmarks are underlined.

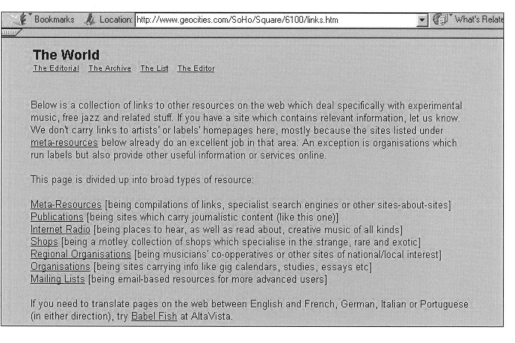

Bookmarks Location: http://www.geocities.com/SoHo/Square/6100/links.htm What's Relate

The World
The Editorial   The Archive   The List   The Editor

Below is a collection of links to other resources on the web which deal specifically with experimental music, free jazz and related stuff. If you have a site which contains relevant information, let us know. We don't carry links to artists' or labels' homepages here, mostly because the sites listed under meta-resources below already do an excellent job in that area. An exception is organisations which run labels but also provide other useful information or services online.

This page is divided up into broad types of resource:

Meta-Resources [being compilations of links, specialist search engines or other sites-about-sites]
Publications [being sites which carry journalistic content (like this one)]
Internet Radio [being places to hear, as well as read about, creative music of all kinds]
Shops [being a motley collection of shops which specialise in the strange, rare and exotic]
Regional Organisations [being musicians' co-operatives or other sites of national/local interest]
Organisations [being sites carrying info like gig calendars, studies, essays etc]
Mailing Lists [being email-based resources for more advanced users]

If you need to translate pages on the web between English and French, German, Italian or Portuguese (in either direction), try Babel Fish at AltaVista.

Putting your site together ....

Using bookmarks like these is an extremely helpful way to organise a longer page. Of course, if each of these sections were a screen or two long, you might also consider splitting them up into separate pages.

The essential email link

Every web site should have, somewhere, an email link enabling visitors to contact the person who created it. After all, sharing your information is all well and good, but it's nice to receive other people's information and comments, too. What's more, an email link enables visitors to report problems with your site, which is invaluable.

To do this, you use a special kind of link, like this:

<p> If you have any more information about the history of the
Paris Metro, please <a href = 'mailto:richard@internet-handbooks.
co.uk'>
email me</a>.</p>

Of course, you should replace 'richard@internet-handbooks.co.uk' with your email address. It's good style to provide your email address on the index page, and many sites provide a 'mailto:' link on every page (you can put it in the template), sometimes in a form like this:

<p> <font size='1'>This site is created and maintained by
<a href='mailto:richard@internet-handbooks.co.uk'>Richard Co-
chrane</a>.
</font></p>

Using this small, unobtrusive line of text on each page means that visitors can instantly respond to anything they see, anywhere on your site. It's also helpful to type out your email address somewhere on the site because not everyone has software which is suitable for the 'mailto' link. One solution is this:

<p> <font size='1'>This site is edited by Richard Cochrane
(<a href='mailto:richard@internet-handbooks.co.uk'>
richard@internet-handbooks.co.uk</a>).</font></p>

It's not terribly elegant, but it makes your page a bit more user-friendly.

Creating a special email address
It is strongly recommended that you use a different email address for your web site from the one you use for everyday correspondence. The sad fact is that publishing your email address on the web makes it available to all kinds of unscrupulous people who will sell it on to direct-marketing companies, some of which can be rather sleazy. You can get a free, web-based email account from any of these companies:

http://www.yahoo.com
http://www.hotmail.com
http://www.mail.com
http://www.jahoopa.com

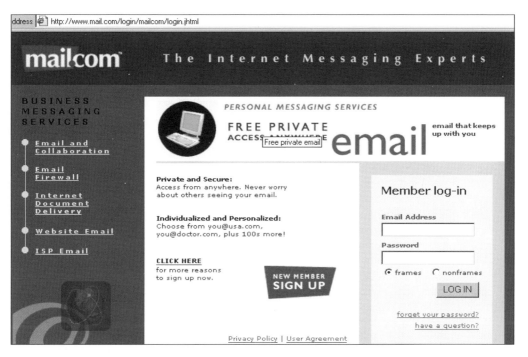

Choosing a smaller, less well-known company gives you a better chance of getting the name you want. For example, it would be hard for me to be 'richard@somemail.com' if Somemail has millions of users; someone is bound to have picked 'richard' already. I would have a better chance with a smaller company. Type 'free email' into any search engine and shop around for a cool name if it's important to you. Also, note that many people use a nickname or the title of their site as their email name, so you might find it easier to be IloveJS@internet-handbooks.co.uk instead.

Fig. 31. Mail.com is one of hundreds of web sites offering free email accounts. Signing up takes just a few minutes. Email accounts like these are very simple to use.

▶ Never, ever, put your private home address, telephone or fax number on your web site. If somebody wants to send you something, let them contact you by email first. It's standard practice throughout the web. It's not a good idea to publish that kind of information indiscriminately, even if your site is advertising a home business. I run a music site, and of course I have many record labels writing to me asking where they can send CDs for review. Nobody expects to find the address on the site.

Testing your new site

Once you've created all of your pages, it's time to test them out. Again, make sure that all of the graphics and other files are in a single directory (folder) on your hard drive, along with your HTML pages, before you start.

Now open the index page in your browser and follow every link on every page, checking for the following:

Putting your site together ....

Has something strange happened?
If your text isn't displaying properly, or the links don't work, look at the HTML for tags or inverted commas you may have forgotten to close. It is very easy to type, say, <a href='menu.html> Menu </a>, and this will have dramatic consequences.

Does the page look the way I want it to?
If not, it is not too late to change elements of the design, especially if you don't have too many pages. It's worth getting it right before you go public.

Have all of the graphics appeared?
If not, make sure the <img src> attribute is set correctly. Make sure the image is in the same directory (folder) as the rest of your site.

Does the page load up almost instantly?
If you have to wait more than two or three seconds for a page to load from your hard drive, it's going to take a lot longer over the internet. Consider reducing the number or the size of your graphics. Make sure you have compressed each graphics file as much as you can.

Is the site logical? Will your imaginary visitor find it easy to get around?
If not, think about adding more links. Or, think about adding descriptions to your links so that people will understand them easily.

If you have the time – and it can be time well spent – test the site in a number of different browsers and browser versions. At the time of writing, these are the most useful ones:

Internet Explorer 5	Netscape Navigator 4
America Online 5	Internet Explorer 3

As new versions come out, keep yourself up to date, but keep the older versions as well, because most people don't update their browser very often.

There's a saying among web designers that no page is foolproof unless it's been tested on all kinds of exotic browsers like Opera, NetCaptor and Lynx. The truth is that the vast majority of non-technical users will be viewing your page through one of the ones listed above. America Online subscribers use the proprietary AOL browser – there are more than 25 million AOL users. All these browsers are downloadable from their main web sites, or from many software archives. Remember that they are large files which will take a while to download, but if you want to be certain that 90 per cent of visitors will see exactly what you intend, then it's worth it.

Testing on several browsers is particularly important if your pages are very 'designed', and if the look of your pages is important to you. If you are basically using text with a few graphics, there is no need to test so extensively. The HTML you have learned from this book is clean and

simple, and it can be read by any browser worth its salt. Just remember that there might be a few variations for people using different software.

Fig. 32. Browserwatch is one of several places online where you can explore current trends in browser usage and capabilities.

6 Going live

In this chapter we will explore:

▶ *finding a free hosting service for your web site*
▶ *joining a hosting service*
▶ *getting your web pages online*
▶ *visiting your new site*
▶ *using a counter to collect statistics about visitors*

Finding a free hosting service for your web site

Now you have your web site designed and ready for the world to look at, it's time to publish it so that other internet users can see it. For this, you will need to use a hosting service. Web site hosting was once an expensive consideration, but today home-pagers can get their sites hosted free in exchange for carrying some advertising for the host company.

Hosting services
A hosting service is a company which has massive amounts of disk space on machines which are connected to the internet as 'web servers'. If your web site is hosted on one of these machines, it will have a special address which web users can type in to see your site. Maybe you have seen home pages with addresses like this:

http://www.geocities.com/soho/square/6100

Well, that's a site hosted by Yahoo/Geocities, one of the largest free web hosting services around at the time of writing. Literally millions of people have hosted their personal web pages at Geocities over the last four or five years.

Fewer things on the web are free any more. 'Free' hosting normally means that your page will have to carry advertising which the hosting service sells. That's how they make their money. If you don't want advertising on your page, you will need to pay for a 'premium' service instead. Fortunately, free hosting services usually offer such a service as an upgrade, so you can try them out for free first, and then pay if you want to.

How to find a hosting service
The first step is to find a hosting service you want to use. Your own internet service provider may well offer a free personal web hosting service; all the big ones do – America Online, CompuServe, Freeserve, Demon, Virgin, and many others. Aside from these, here are some of the best-known services to get you started:

http://www.geocities.com

http://www.tripod.com

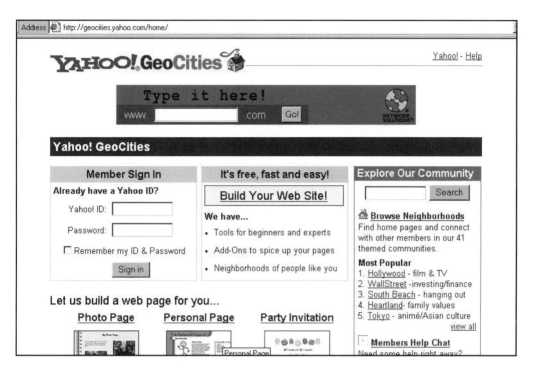

http://www.fortunecity.co.uk

http://www.talkcity.com

Fig. 33. At the time of writing, Geocities has become one of the largest free hosting services on the web. Originally independent, it is now part of the fast-growing Yahoo! network of companies.

Content guidelines
Web hosts usually publish a set of content guidelines. Take a quick look at these to be sure you that won't be infringing their guidelines with the site you intend to upload. Different services have different rules. For example, there may be prohibitions against commercial web sites, or 'adult materi- al', or other possibly offensive content. You will probably be able to locate a service somewhere which suits you, whatever your subject matter.

Advertising
Visit some of their members' pages and see what you think. Ask yourself:

1. How does the advertising appear? Is it annoying, or fairly low key? Many sites choose to carry extra advertising. Look for a banner or pop-up window that appears on every site this service hosts. Many hosts offer a choice between pop-up windows and a less intrusive banner embedded in the page.

2. Are all sites obliged to carry a logo or other gizmo that tells visitors who the host is? Is this acceptable to you, or would it spoil the look of your pages?

Advertising is a fact of life on the web today. It isn't going to disappear, so just try to find a host that suits you. Some smaller hosts require less advertising from home-pagers, so don't automatically go for the biggest name you can find.

Also, remember that you are storing your web site on your own hard drive. You can move it to another host whenever you want. So long as you keep all your original files safely, there is no danger of 'losing' your site if you later decide to move to a different hosting service.

Joining a hosting service

All hosting services require you to 'join'. This will enable you to get a password, and an address (URL) for your new site. The procedure is usually very simple. If it isn't, the site is badly designed. Just fill in an online form with your details and click a button. You should be given (or allowed to choose) an address for your web site.

Disclosing personal information
It is entirely up to *you* to decide what information to give to any internet service. Disclosing personal details such as annual income, sex, age and marital status ought to be optional, but sometimes it isn't. The reason is that services on the web often sell their demographic data to marketing companies. If you don't want this to happen, there's no reason why you should be scrupulously truthful here. For legitimate reasons of personal privacy and data protection, a high proportion of internet users enter fictional names and addresses.

▶ *Tip* – Never provide a correct physical address or non-business telephone number on the internet unless the service offers a 'secure transmission'. Even trustworthy sources can be hacked, after all. This is particularly true if your site has any potentially controversial contents.

At this stage, be sure to write down the following information, which the host service should confirm to you once you've finished registering:

1. your URL (web site address)

2. your username

3. your password

You will also probably receive a free email address, and you will probably want to make a note of that, too.

The URL (uniform resource locator) will be the address of your web site. It's the bit that comes after 'http://' in the location (address) bar of your readers' browsers.

Getting your web pages online

Preparing your files
The next thing to do is to copy ('upload') your web site onto the host's server. Your site will then be accessible to the rest of the world. Before doing this:

1. Check that you have saved all the files needed by your site in a single

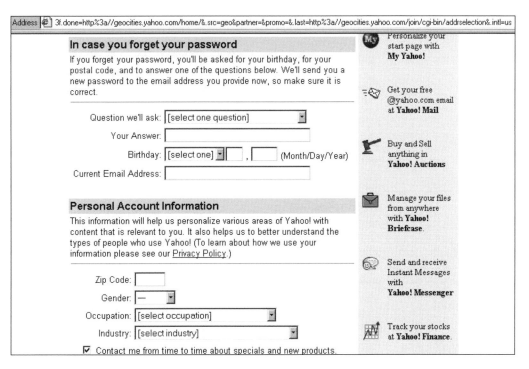

Address 3f.done=http%3a//geocities.yahoo.com/home/&.src=geo&partner=&promo=&.last=http%3a//geocities.yahoo.com/join/cgi-bin/addrselection&.intl=us

Fig. 34. Opening a new account with a web hosting service is as easy as filling in a form like this one.

directory (folder) on your hard drive. Give the folder a name such as 'Mywebsite'.

2. It is also a good idea to delete or move any dummy files, abandoned files, notes and so on, from that folder.

3. Check the filenames of your web pages and images. There can be no blank spaces in file names on the internet, as there can be on a personal computer. If you want to denote a space in a filename, you could use an underscore. For example:

my_web_page.html

File Transfer Protocol without tears
Files like web pages and images are transferred from one computer's hard disk to another by using file transfer protocol or FTP. Many host services have a web-based file manager which helps you to upload your files, and you should investigate this first. They tend to be especially useful for web sites with a fairly small number of files (say twenty or so, including image files such as GIFs and JPGs).

Finding some popular FTP software
However, it's always faster, and often easier, to use a special FTP 'client' program to handle this for you. One of the most popular at the time of writing is called WS_FTP. This is available from moat software download sites. Use a search engine to search for 'ws_ftp.zip' (the name of the file you need to download) if you are having trouble. The download should be very quick. The company that makes it is called Ipswitch.com. Other

well-known packages include Voyager and CuteFTP. They all work in a very similar way, and are found on the CD ROMs supplied with the monthly computer and internet magazines, as well as being available as downloads from the internet.

CuteFTP
http://www.cuteftp.com/
The popular software utility from GlobalScape.

FTP Voyager
http://www.ftpvoyager.com/
Looks and handles very like Windows Explorer.

WS_FTP95
http://www.ipswitch.com
Quickly and easily uploads and manages your web site. Again, it looks and handles files and folders very like Windows Explorer.

Setting up your FTP client
Your hosting service will provide you with instructions for setting up your FTP client to communicate with their hard disk. It can seem daunting the first time, but in reality it is normally a very brief and painless operation once you've tried it a couple of times. The information you usually need is:

Fig. 35. Transferring files over the internet (FTP) can these days be done using a simple program like WS_FTP. This looks and feels very much like the Windows Explorer software with which most people are now familiar.

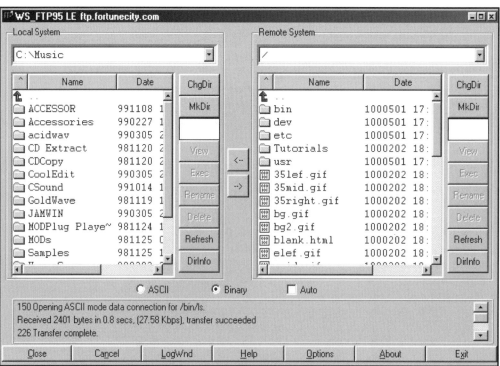

1. Host address. You will be advised of this by your web hosting service. It could be a form of words something like one of these:

    ftp.geocities.com (for Geocities home-pagers)
    upload.virgin.net (for Virgin Net home-pagers)

2. User ID (your username on the hosting service).

3. Password.

Sometimes you might also need to specify these settings:

(a) The Port number. This is usually 21. If not, your hosting service should tell you which one it is.

(b) Network timeout. You could try about 65 seconds. Make it longer if you get a lot of error messages saying the connection 'timed out'.

(c) Host machine type. Your hosting service will have to tell you this. Most FTP clients will automatically figure it out for you anyway. If in doubt, just click Autodetect or similar option.

Usually, though, your FTP client will handle all of the above information for you.

Uploading your files using the FTP client
Once you have connected to the internet, open up your FTP client software. Start the FTP connection. The client software will then display a file management window. Here, you select files from your own (local) computer and copy them onto the host's (remote) computer. This is usually how it is done:

1. You browse for your web page files on your (local) computer, in one part of the window.

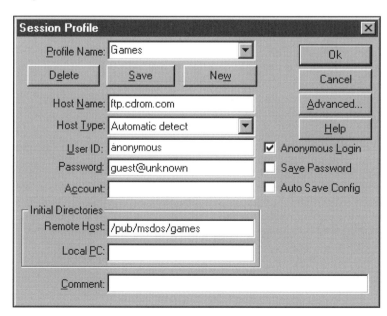

Fig. 36. Filling in the information which WS_FTP requires might look confusing at first, but your host will provide you with the three or four essential details you need.

2. Highlight all the files you want to upload.

3. Double-click on them to upload them (or click on a button saying Upload, Send or similar).

4. When uploaded, the filenames magically appear in another part of the window, which represents your web (remote) host. This shows you that the process of uploading is completed.

The uploading usually only takes a few seconds per file. The speed of uploading will depend in part on the time of day, and the amount of internet traffic. Once it's done your site is published on the web. It's that simple!

Visiting your new site

Now close your FTP client, or log out of the web-based file manager if that's what you were using. Type your new URL into the location (address) panel in your browser, and there's your index page. Anyone in the world who knows your URL can do the same, and they will see exactly what you are seeing now. Your web site has been published.

Carrying out a check
It's time to check that everything is present and correct by going through your site again, just as you did when it was only on your hard drive. It's amazing how easy it is to miss out an image or page when transferring a site by FTP. The only way you'll know is by taking the time to systematically check every single link on every page.

Updating your pages
Most hosting services offer a way for you to edit your pages online. You might like to try this out too, but remember that you can always edit on your hard disk and upload later. This is usually better for complicated changes because it reduces the amount of time you will need to spend online.

▶ *Tip* – If you edit pages online, remember to also update the version on your hard drive. That way, when you make changes to the version on your hard drive, you won't be over-writing useful things like the code for including your counter on the page.

Adding a counter

One thing worth doing right away is to add a counter to your index page. This is a little gadget which counts the number of times the page has been visited. Perhaps you've seen pages with a line saying 'This site has been visited 0006554 times' or something similar. Well, there's no need to display your counter to the world, but knowing how many visits you've had is extremely useful, especially when your site is new.

Where to get a counter
Most web hosting services offer their own counter, and one counter is as

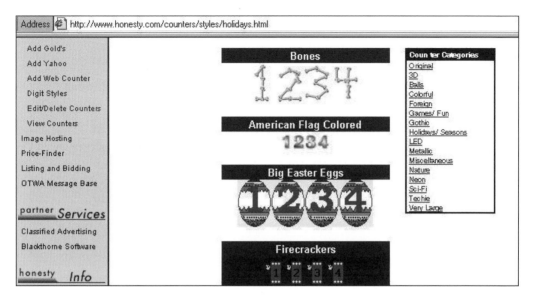

good as another unless you particularly care what it looks like. Remember, it doesn't have to be visible – in fact, most professional web sites don't show their counters. Rest assured, however, that the counters are there, in the background, letting them measure how successful their site is at attracting visitors.

A counter is a piece of software which you can find in various places on the web. You simply need to register to use one, often by filling in an online form. You then insert a little piece of HTML into your index page. Whoever is providing the counter will explain exactly what the HTML should look like. You can probably just copy and paste it straight in.

If your host doesn't supply a counter, or you'd like to try a different one, there are plenty around. Here are a few URLs to start you off:

http://ultimatecounter.com/

http://www.pagecount.com/

http://www.thecounter.com/

http://www.webstat.net

For now, insert the HTML into the version of your index page on your hard drive, then FTP the amended index page to the host. It will automatically overwrite the old version.

Using a statistical service
A counter usually records the number of times a page has been opened (so-called 'page impressions'). If your index page is a main menu, which readers return to often while navigating your site, you may well find that one visitor increases your count by more than one point. Simple counters provide a rough idea of how popular your site is, but they don't give you any detailed breakdown.

Fig. 37. Most web sites hide their counters, but free services like Honesty.com's offer a wide range of styles to choose from, including these rather frivolous-looking ones.

It's possible to get a lot of information about your visitors using a counter, but normally these statistical services cost money. It's not worth considering a statistical service right away, but you might want to think about it as your site begins to attract visitors. Some of the things a decent statistical service will provide you with are:

1. Numbers of individual visitors.
2. Details of which browsers your visitors are using.
3. Numbers of visitors per day, week or month, or even per hour.
4. Average amount of time spent at your site.
5. Details of the web site they visited immediately before arriving at yours.

As you can see, this is going to be useful when you've started to promote your site and you are getting a fair number of visits, but there is no need to worry about it immediately.

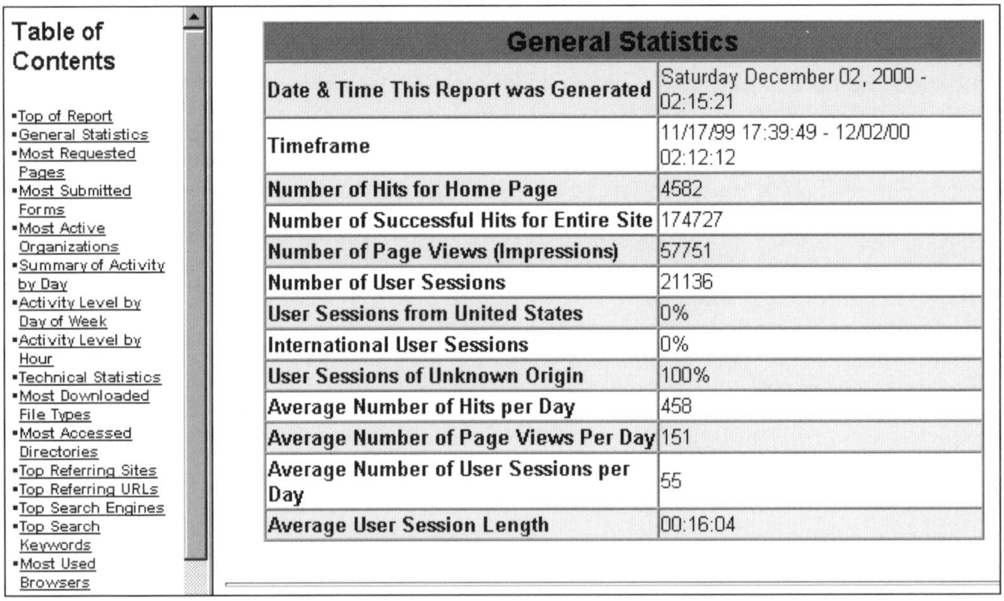

Table of Contents

- Top of Report
- General Statistics
- Most Requested Pages
- Most Submitted Forms
- Most Active Organizations
- Summary of Activity by Day
- Activity Level by Day of Week
- Activity Level by Hour
- Technical Statistics
- Most Downloaded File Types
- Most Accessed Directories
- Top Referring Sites
- Top Referring URLs
- Top Search Engines
- Top Search Keywords
- Most Used Browsers

General Statistics	
Date & Time This Report was Generated	Saturday December 02, 2000 - 02:15:21
Timeframe	11/17/99 17:39:49 - 12/02/00 02:12:12
Number of Hits for Home Page	4582
Number of Successful Hits for Entire Site	174727
Number of Page Views (Impressions)	57751
Number of User Sessions	21136
User Sessions from United States	0%
International User Sessions	0%
User Sessions of Unknown Origin	100%
Average Number of Hits per Day	458
Average Number of Page Views Per Day	151
Average Number of User Sessions per Day	55
Average User Session Length	00:16:04

Fig. 38. An example of the kind of statistical information available from a commercial organisation such as Webtrends.

7 Attracting visitors

In this chapter we will explore:

- ▶ *search engines*
- ▶ *thinking of key words*
- ▶ *using meta tags*
- ▶ *registering your site with search engines*
- ▶ *Yahoo! – a special case*
- ▶ *improving your search engine listings*
- ▶ *promotion beyond the search engines*
- ▶ *getting your web site bookmarked*
- ▶ *printed matter*
- ▶ *mutual links*
- ▶ *creating a links page*
- ▶ *internet mailing lists*
- ▶ *encouraging other sites to link to yours*
- ▶ *promoting your site on mailing lists and Usenet*

Search engines

Why has nobody come?
If you put a counter on your index page and then leave it for a while, you may be in for a surprise. It is very likely that nobody has visited your site at all. In theory your web site has a potential audience of hundreds of millions of users, but unless you help them to find it they will never visit.

The truth is, once your web site is published on the internet, your job has only just begun. Fortunately, the process of promoting your site can be fun and educational.

Search engines
The most popular way for people to find web sites is through search engines. A search engine or internet directory is a web site that acts as a directory of other sites. As the name implies, it enables users to search for sites on subjects that interest them. If you haven't used a search engine before, visit some of these popular ones to get an idea of how they work:

About.com
http://home.about.com

Alta Vista
http://www.altavista.com

Excite
http://www.excite.com

Google
http://www.google.com

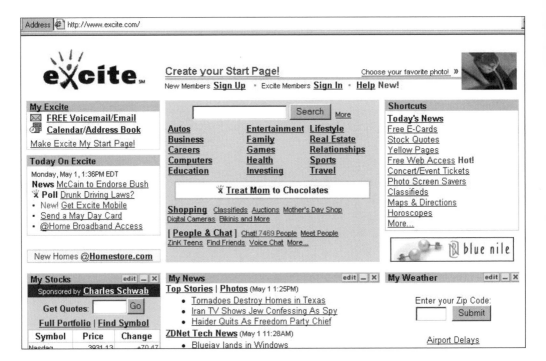

Address 🔎 http://www.excite.com/

Fig. 39. Excite is one of the largest search engines and internet directories. Its front page looks as you might expect, with helpful subject categories, special promotions and that all-important little search box to type in what you are looking for.

Infoseek
http://www.infoseek.com

UK Plus
http://www.ukplus.co.uk

Yahoo!
http://www.yahoo.com

You'll notice how different all these popular sites are, but they all share these things in common:

1. Each holds a massive list of millions of web sites.

2. Each allows users to search for web pages by entering key words relating to the subjects they are looking for.

3. Most of them also organise web sites into helpful subject categories.

One way to draw attention to your web site is by registering it with as many search engines as possible. Before you do, however, it's well worth getting your site ready for this so that people can find it more easily. Submitting your site to search engines before it's ready can be a waste of time. Fortunately, getting it ready is not too difficult.

Thinking of keywords

The first step in getting your site ready is to think of some key words or phrases which best describe it. Imagine you're searching for a site like your own – which words would you type into a search engine in order to find it? The first ones which come into your head may well be the first which occur to others, too, so be sure to make a note of them.

You should also, however, include specific phrases in your list. Suppose your site is about American TV show *The Simpsons*. You might think of some words like these:

Simpsons
cartoon
animation
TV
television
comedy
humour

But try typing any of these words into a search engine, and you'll see that there are already hundreds – even thousands – of sites which turn up with these keywords. To beat some of these sites in your potential readers' searches, you need to match either a range of key words or a specific phrase.

Example
Let's say your site includes, among other things, a complete list of guest artists who've appeared on the show over the years. You might include 'guest artist' and 'guest voice' on your list. Someone looking for a list of guest artists who've appeared on *The Simpsons* might well type something like this into a search engine:

+"Simpsons" + "guest artists"

which means that pages from your search must include the word *The Simpsons* and the phrase 'guest artist'.

Thinking of keywords is something of an art form. Here are some pointers:

1. Be as specific as you can.

2. If possible, use obscure words, names or other uncommon but specific search terms.

3. Whole phrases are very powerful – think of as many as possible.

4. Include plurals and alternative spellings wherever appropriate – you might be surprised to learn that the most clued-up sites even include common mis-spellings of their search terms, too.

5. Try to create a picture of what's distinctive about your site from this list. Don't assume that people will be looking for just any site on the subject; assume that your particular site is exactly what they're searching for.

Using meta tags

Once you have got your list of key words, it's time to put them onto your pages. You do this using the < meta / > HTML tag. This goes inside the < head > section of your page, and it can take various different attributes. Let's look at an example set of meta tags:

< meta name='Description' content='Review of Derek Bailey and Steve Lacy CD for Musings online music magazine' / >
< meta name='Keywords' content='improv, improvised music, free improvisation, free improv, guitar, sax, saxophone, Steve Lacy, Lacy, Derek Bailey, free jazz, jazz, improvisation, new jazz' / >

Each of these two < meta / > tags has a name and a content attribute. Notice that the tags don't need a closing < /meta > after them.

These two names mean something specific to different search engines. Many search engines use the content of the tag named 'description' as the text which goes underneath the link to your page on a search results screen.

It's worth knowing that some search engines use the first paragraph of text on your page to decide how relevant it is to any particular search. That means that this section ought to be as punchy and to the point as possible, giving a clear description of what's on the page and including some key words if possible.

The rules used by search engines change all the time as their technology develops. Keep up to date with an industry newsletter like:

Fig. 40. Like most search engines, Excite's results pages show handy summaries of each site found, underneath its title link.

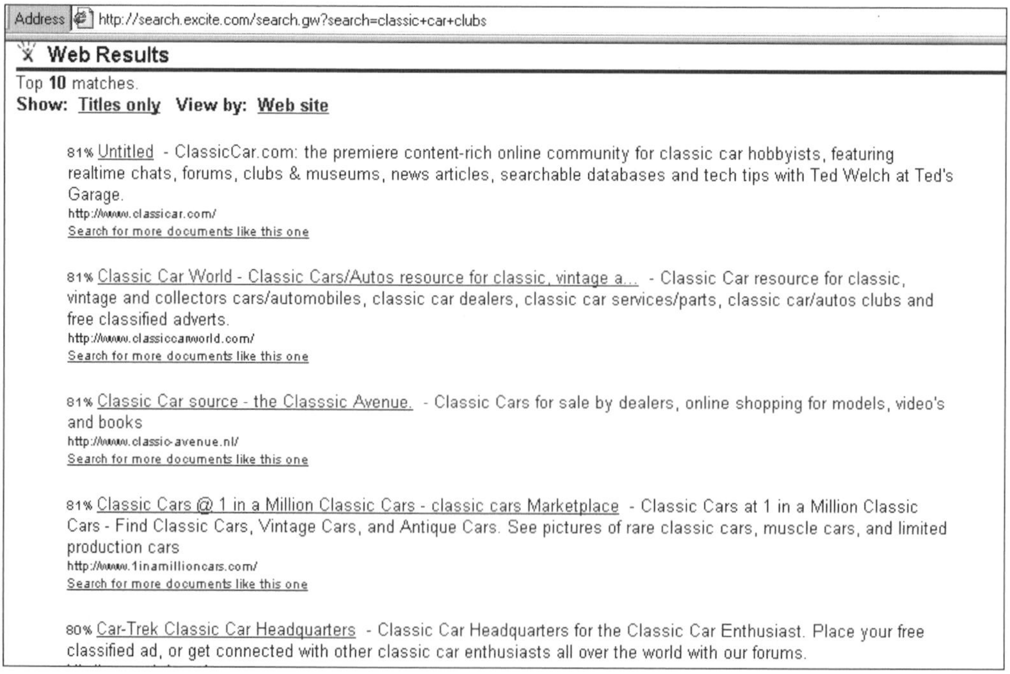

Address 🔲 http://search.excite.com/search.gw?search=classic+car+clubs

Web Results

Top **10** matches.
Show: <u>Titles only</u>   View by: <u>Web site</u>

81% <u>Untitled</u> - ClassicCar.com: the premiere content-rich online community for classic car hobbyists, featuring realtime chats, forums, clubs & museums, news articles, searchable databases and tech tips with Ted Welch at Ted's Garage.
http://www.classicar.com/
<u>Search for more documents like this one</u>

81% <u>Classic Car World - Classic Cars/Autos resource for classic, vintage a...</u> - Classic Car resource for classic, vintage and collectors cars/automobiles, classic car dealers, classic car services/parts, classic car/autos clubs and free classified adverts.
http://www.classiccarworld.com/
<u>Search for more documents like this one</u>

81% <u>Classic Car source - the Classsic Avenue.</u> - Classic Cars for sale by dealers, online shopping for models, video's and books
http://www.classic-avenue.nl/
<u>Search for more documents like this one</u>

81% <u>Classic Cars @ 1 in a Million Classic Cars - classic cars Marketplace</u> - Classic Cars at 1 in a Million Classic Cars - Find Classic Cars, Vintage Cars, and Antique Cars. See pictures of rare classic cars, muscle cars, and limited production cars
http://www.1inamillioncars.com/
<u>Search for more documents like this one</u>

80% <u>Car-Trek Classic Car Headquarters</u> - Classic Car Headquarters for the Classic Car Enthusiast. Place your free classified ad, or get connected with other classic car enthusiasts all over the world with our forums.

All About Search Engines
http://marketing-resources.com/SEzine.html
It is delivered free by email.

Registering your site with search engines

Once the meta tags are in place, you are ready to register your web site
with some search engines. There are three ways of doing this:

1. manually

2. using an automatic submission site

3. using a premium service

Manual submission services
By choosing the first option, you're resigning yourself to spending at least
an afternoon tapping the same basic details into search engine submission forms over and over again. You will need to provide a short
description of your site and your list of keywords along with the things
you probably expect – URL, email address and title of the site, plus some
personal details about yourself.

Automatic submission services
Fortunately, automatic submission services like SubmitIt help take some
of the grind out of getting registered with the major search engines.
Some sites let you input the main information once only, and then send
that information to around two dozen search engines in turn. Some of

Fig. 41. Using SubmitIt
you can submit your site
to 400 of the top search
engines and directories all
in one place, and re-
submit your site
automatically to ensure
you remain listed. The
bCentral service is part of
Microsoft.

these require a little extra information, but this process is much better than the manual one. Here are some well-known automatic submission sites you might consider:

Add URL
http://add-url.hypermart.net/

SubmitIt
http://www.submitit.com/sitrial.htm

Submit Plus
http://submitplus.bc.ca/

In practice, however, these sites don't always offer the exact search engines you want to be registered with, and so you'll use a mixture of automatic and manual submissions for your site's launch.

Finally, you might like to put the icing on the cake by announcing your site on some internet announcement pages. It's hard to say who uses such sites, or what they use them for, but an announcement here can generate a bit of traffic to your site and get people interested, especially if the site is angled towards your area of interest or your target audience. You can find a list of general announcement sites at this Yahoo! page:

http://dir.yahoo.com/Computers_and_Internet/Internet/World_
Wide_Web/Searching_the_Web/Indices_to_Web_Documents/
Free_ for_All_Pages/

Using a premium service
Premium services give you the option of paying someone else to deal with the search engine submission forms on your behalf. They can be pretty cheap or extremely expensive, depending in part on the level of service.

Be warned, however, about parting with money in return for 'guaranteed traffic'. Your site may get plenty of visitors, but they may very well be people who are looking for something entirely different. How many times have you seen search results that didn't match what you were looking for? Some of these will have been mistakes. Others may have been trying to entice you into clicking on the links so that your visit counts as a 'hit' to the page, even if you immediately click the Back button and try something else.

Also, be aware that promises to get your site listed in 500 or 600 search engines are probably not much use to you. The overwhelming majority of net users are only using the top dozen or so search sites – not these obscure or specialist ones which might not even be suitable for your home page. Unless your web site is part of a business plan and includes a budget for promoting the site, it's probably not worth the expense. And anyway, isn't the web site itself supposed to be a promotional tool? If it is doing its job properly, why would you need to spend money advertising it?

Yahoo! – a special case

At the time of writing, Yahoo! is probably the single most powerful brand on the web. Its web directory (a kind of organised search engine) was the beginning of that empire, and it is still massively popular.

To get listed in Yahoo!, however, you have to do more than just fill in a form. Sites are only listed in Yahoo! if they pass muster when inspected by a human being, a member of the Yahoo! staff who checks out their functionality and quality.

Yahoo!-approved sites are not necessarily flash, corporate brochures full of cool graphics and animations and suchlike. What Yahoo! seems most keen on is three things:

1.   Some content, not just a collection of links to other sites.

2.   Reasonable layout and design.

3.   A site whose subject will fit into Yahoo!'s (very extensive) directory structure.

Once you've launched your site, lodge a request with Yahoo! that they have a look at it. It can't hurt. If they turn you down, don't worry – you will be in extremely good company. Just work on the site a bit more and go back to them again.

A listing in Yahoo! will really help your traffic. Try to get your site in a section of the directory which isn't already very full; that will make yours stand out more clearly. You can suggest your site to Yahoo! at this page:

Yahoo! Suggest a Site
http://docs.yahoo.com/info/suggest

Fig. 42. This is the page for Yahoo!'s Suggest a Site service. You can suggest your own web site here.

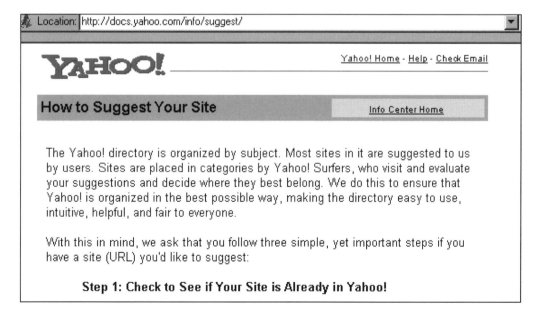

87

Promotion beyond the search engines

Having said all of this about search engines, the truth is that most web traffic doesn't come directly from such places. That surprises a lot of people, including regular web users, but how many of the telephone numbers you dial in a week have been looked up in the phone book? Probably not many. You probably got the numbers from one of three places:

1. your address book

2. a brochure, flyer, menu, business card or other printed matter

3. a friend or colleague

Getting your web site bookmarked

The first of these is similar to the Favourites or Bookmarks of useful web sites which people collect in their web browsers. The ones that are best at attracting traffic are those which are best at persuading people to bookmark them for future use. Odd though it may sound, most web sites attract far more of their visitors from bookmarks than from anywhere else.

▶ *Key point* – the only real way to encourage people to bookmark your site and return to it is by presenting good-quality content and updating it regularly.

Printed matter

This is something this book can't really help with, except that if you have printed business cards, letterheads, Christmas cards or anything else, do make sure you include your new URL if it's a business site. If not, you should send emails to any of your friends who might be interested, including the URL. Most email programs nowadays allow users to click on a URL in a message and immediately see the site (you've probably seen this). Encourage your friends to send the address to anyone who might be interested. Word of mouth can be your best ally.

Mutual links

Mutual links are a source of URLs which is hugely valuable, and probably the most important source of so-called 'hidden web traffic'. This is the backbone of a long-standing web site's underlying traffic, the people who visit every month whether any particular promotion has gone on or not.

Let's say you visit a site about bodybuilding to look for information about the Mr Olympia tournament (it could happen); you go to www.muscle.com but that site deals mostly with training tips and example workouts. Their site, however, also has a link to www.pro-bodybuilding.com, which looks much more promising.

This interconnectedness between different sites is what makes the web so useful, and it can turn the much-ridiculed idea of surfing from site to site into an extremely quick way to find the information you want. You need to get your site into this network, this web of connections. Get a link from a site that has 100,000 visitors a month and even if only one per cent of their visitors click on your link, that's 1,000 a month from that site alone. You need some mutual links.

Mutual links are so called because, since everyone wants more links from sites, and since the more traffic they get, the better it is for everyone, it's in everyone's interest to link to each other. So here's how you get some mutual links:

1. Find some sites which are similar to yours in subject-matter. Use anything from very professional sites to home-made ones, as long as you're happy to be associated with them.

2. In each case, make a note of the email address of the person who makes or maintains it. You can usually copy and paste this into your text editor, rather than writing it down by hand like some character from a Dickens novel.

3. Send an email to each person saying something like this:

> Hi, I just visited your site and thought it was really funny/cool/ useful. I've put in a link to it from the site I run about The Simpsons/ interior design/flute-playing. Come and visit some time, I'm at http://www.freehomepages.com/somehomepageorother. Of course, if you'd like to link to this site, I'd be grateful. Let me know what you think.

This kind of message is polite and acknowledges that you're asking the person who runs the other site for a favour. They'll probably be so pleased you linked to them and said something nice that – as long as your site is relevant and not too terrible – they may well agree.

Don't send this type of email to a list of several people. That's lazy, and it will get you ignored. You may have only one chance to make a good impression with the people who currently have all the web traffic in your subject area, so be nice and try to give them something in return (i.e. the wonderful new content on your site).

Creating a links page

Many sites, including some of my own, have a links page. As its name implies, this is a page which contains only links to other sites. There are few things more irritating than sites which are nothing but links pages, but such a page, strictly as an additional extra to your site, can be extremely useful. A really good links page is the kind of thing people will bookmark and use as a jumping-off point when looking for all kinds of information about your subject.

Try to get a mutual link from every site on your links page, but don't worry if someone says 'no' or ignores your email. People can be like that.

Also, some sites just won't link to anyone who doesn't pay them. List them anyway. It makes your site better because your links page should really be as complete as possible, and they may change their mind when word gets out about your great site (this may take a while, so be patient).

Internet mailing lists

One of the oldest forms of internet use is the mailing list. It's a simple idea:

1. Take a group of people who are all interested in, say, T. S. Eliot.

2. One of these people wants to know whether there's a new German translation of *Murder in the Cathedral.*

3. She sends an email to a computer somewhere in Arizona (say). Because she's a member of the group, the computer accepts it.

4. This computer (called a listserver) has a list of email addresses of everyone in the group. It sends her email to every single one of them.

5. Most members of the group ignore it because they're too busy or they don't know the answer.

6. But someone does know, and sends a reply – again, to the computer, so that everyone in the group gets to see it.

In most mailing lists, this would be a fairly typical scenario:

(a) A third person claims that the translation referred to is rubbish, and an earlier one is much better.

(b) The person who originally answered gets annoyed, and replies rather huffily.

(c) Several more people jump in. The argument now splits into several bits. Some are calmly discussing the merits of the different editions. Some have got into a discussion of translation in general. The others are just abusing each other.

(d) Unaccountably, the subject suddenly goes dead, and everyone loses interest. Those who didn't send a single email have probably learned the most, but everyone learned something, if only that picking fights on mailing lists is rarely a productive use of their time.

Yes, mailing lists can be unpredictable, eccentric, downright idiosyncratic things. Some are 'moderated', which means that someone is nominally in charge, and is supposed to stop people from ranging off-topic and swearing at one another. In practice, lists which are gently but not too heavily moderated are the most fun. Unless it specifically says so in their information, mailing lists are not great places for the easily offended or the very young, as ideas are often expressed forcefully and egos go into battle with numbing regularity.

If all this hasn't put you off, mailing lists are one of the best places to promote a web site.

Finding and joining mailing lists
Finding mailing lists is easy enough. Look by subject on Liszt:

Liszt
http://www.liszt.com
This is the largest and one of the oldest sources of mailing list info on the net, with more than 90,000 different mailing lists on offer.

Joining a mailing list is different depending on the type of list – that is, depending on the software running on the machine which does the work. Generally speaking, you will send an email from the account where you receive mail saying something like 'subscribe jazz-l Richard Cochrane', but check out the information first.

   Most list services offer you the option of a 'digest mode'. Instead of sending you each mail as it comes in, the machine will bundle a whole day's messages into a single email and send them to you the next day (roughly speaking). High-volume mailing lists can zoom up to over a hundred messages a day, and most of them may be of little interest, so if your mailbox is getting crammed, check whether you can go over to this method instead.

   Some lists are just 'dead'. They may have many signed-up members, but nobody talks about anything. Trying to start a conversation on a list like this can be like dropping pebbles down a deep, dark well. Don't persist for too long; look elsewhere instead. The fact is that many of the members may no longer use their signed-up email account any more.

Fig. 43. The home page of Liszt. It has established itself as the biggest and best-known source of mailing lists on the internet.

Mailing list promotion

So, how do you use mailing lists to promote your site? Well, the best way to irritate your newly joined list is to post them all an unsolicited advertisement. Don't send the list a message saying 'Visit my site, the best place to find blah blah blah'. Some lists tolerate this kind of thing, but only barely. You will get extremely unfriendly emails if you do it in the wrong places – and sometimes worse; computer viruses have been known to arrive in the mailboxes of those who use what many regard as a beautiful example of democratic debate as if it were a free advertising hoarding.

Instead, use these two guaranteed techniques to attract interest:

1. Engage with discussions on the list, especially if you can answer people's questions and hence establish yourself as an 'expert'. Always, always include the URL of your site at the bottom of your message, after you've signed off. Most email programs enable you to set a 'signature' which is appended to the bottom of every email you send: if you use one, consider including your URL. You might also include information about recent updates and so on, but keep it to a maximum of four lines of text.

2. When something is discussed which is relevant to your site, refer readers to the site as part of the discussion.

If you can find a few mailing lists which indulge in lively discussion about your site's subject area, these two techniques together will prove both extremely successful and perfectly painless. It's fun to discuss your interests with others, and while you do it you'll be promoting your site as well.

Starting your own mailing list

This used to be rather hard to do. You had to go begging to someone with a mail server running the right kind of software – almost certainly someone at a university, which may or may not be the best place to find someone prepared to host a list about cross-stitch or birdwatching. They would probably say 'no', and you could forget the whole thing.

Nowadays, with web-based services of all kinds developing everywhere, it's easy. Setting up a mailing list is similar to getting a web-based email account: just provide a few details and it's done. Here are some places to do it:

http://www.onelist.com

http://www.listbot.com

http://www.milomail.com

Now what should you do with it? Well, there are at least two ways to use it:

1. As a forum for discussion, like a traditional mailing list. The danger here is that your list will be a dud and no one will want to talk about any-

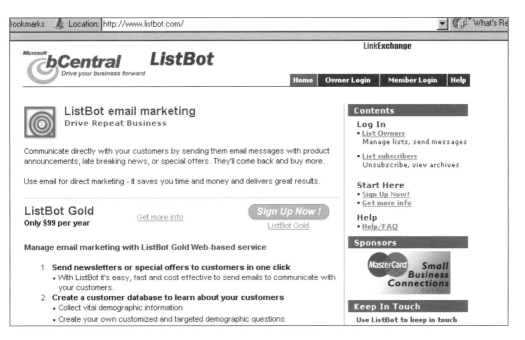

Fig. 44. Listbot is a commercial service from Microsoft for people wanting to set up and run their own internet mailing lists.

thing. The payoff is that members will be constantly reminded about your site as they indulge in one of humanity's favourite activities: arguing about things which probably are not all that important.

2. As an announcement service. Here, you send a mail whenever you update your site, letting people know about new features you've added. This is sometimes called an 'opt-in newsletter'. Most make-your-own-list sites enable you to decide whether other people can post to the list or not, so you can make it like a proper newsletter or a mixture of newsletter and discussion area. You decide.

Whatever you do:

(a) Never add someone's address to your mailing list without obtaining their permission.

(b) Never pester people on other lists to join yours (instead, they should be able to sign up from your site – when you create your list, you should be told how to make this happen).

(c) Never pass your list of members' email addresses to someone else, whoever they are.

More Internet Handbooks to help you

David Holland, *Exploring Yahoo! on the Internet*
Graham Jones, *Promoting Your Web Site on the Internet*
Kye Valongo, *Using Discussion Forums on the Internet*

8 Moving to the next level

In this chapter we will explore:

▶ *redesigning your web site*

▶ *embedding sounds and moving images in your pages*

▶ *adding animated GIFs to your pages*

▶ *adding sound to your pages*

▶ *other files for downloading*

▶ *creating image maps*

▶ *the future of web authoring*

. . . .

Redesigning your web site

Why make your site more complicated?
Over time, you will probably find yourself wanting to change your site's original design. A web site is something which evolves. Rather than expecting to get it right first time, you probably expect to develop it as you learn more about the web.

Redesigning can mean many things, and there are various reasons why you might want to do it:

1. Perhaps you could communicate more information with sounds or moving images.

2. You probably want your site to look more professional.

3. You may find that multimedia elements give your site more identity.

4. Interactive elements can tempt visitors to come back.

5. You may just fancy a change.

Smart redesigning
Redesigning an existing web site can be a big job. Every page has to be changed separately. Making this process potentially less painful begins with some common sense:

(a) Experiment with your designs using one typical page.

(b) When you have it right, look carefully at how the new HTML differs from the original version.

(c) Try to reuse graphics, table layouts and heading formats as much as you can. This tends to look better as well as making a lot less work for you.

If you know how, you can copy and paste your HTML into a programmable word processor like Microsoft Word and then write or record a macro that will take in your changes. You then paste the resulting text back into your text editor.

Microsoft Word, for example, supports macros written in a language called Visual Basic for Applications. While it involves a steep learning curve for non-programmers, it will certainly save you time in the long run. For each page, you would just drop it into the word processor and run the macro. Even if you know what you're doing, you may experience some headaches using this method, but if you have a 100-page site it will be a lot quicker than making all the changes by hand.

Embedding sounds and moving images in your pages

When you look at some of the more advanced things you can do with a web site, your first instinct might be to try to include everything. Rein it in. There are far too many sites out there whose useful content is obscured by a welter of animations, sounds and mini-applications. Ask yourself some searching questions about any new element you are considering:

1.   Does it improve the quality of the site?

2.   Does it add richness to the information you are presenting?

3.   Does it add a fun element which will make visitors want to come back?

If the answer is 'no', leave well alone. Why? The answer is simple: bandwidth. This refers to the demands that your pages make on the poor system of telephone lines that currently carry the bulk of internet traffic. More multimedia requires more bandwidth, and for your visitors more bandwidth means more waiting. How many times have you got fed up waiting for a page to load up, and clicked away to some other page?

Remember, when you are testing web pages, that your hard drive offers a great deal more bandwidth than the average web connection. Pages which load up quickly from your hard drive might not work so well online. If in doubt, upload a test page onto your site and then try to view it yourself. Compare the results using a wristwatch or clock with a second hand.

Embedded or downloadable content?
There are two different ways of presenting people with bandwidth-hungry content:

1.   Incorporate such content on the page, so they see/hear it right away (embedded content).

2.   Give people the option of downloading it and viewing/hearing it on their own hard drive (downloadable content)

In this writer's opinion the second option is much better. The web is not television. It is unable to present moving images and sound smoothly and quickly to those who may be only casually interested. Multimedia demands time and money from your audience, and if you disappoint them – or if they suspect they will be disappointed – they will soon leave.

Moving to the next level ....

Adding animated GIFs to your pages

Animated GIFs are a wonderfully simple way to make your pages more dynamic without expecting your readers to make a cup of tea while waiting for them to load up. An animated GIF is a single GIF file which contains a series of images and instructions about what order to play them in, how quickly, and whether to loop them indefinitely.

Animation software
You need a piece of software to create animated GIFs. The following are good ones:

Animagic
http://rtlsoft.com/animagic

Gamani
http://www.gamani.com

Mind Workshop
http://www.mindworkshop.com/alchemy/gifcon.html

Web Utilities
http://www.webutilities.com/products/GAni/runme.htm

Fig. 45. AniMagic lets you load up a series of images, and then arrange them to create an animation of your own.

Generally, you tell the software which graphics to use to create the animation, and then save it with a new name. Creating the separate 'frames' of the animation is the hardest bit. If your graphics skills aren't too strong, remember that an animated GIF need not be a cartoon-like animation. Try some very simple ideas. For example, you could create

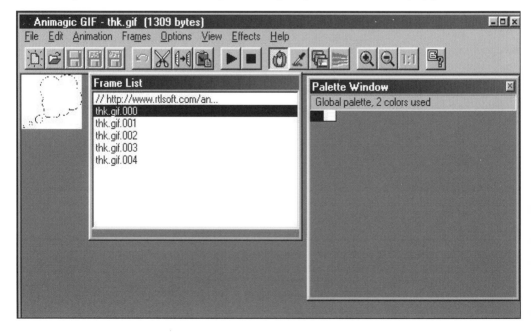

words whose letters change colour or flash on and off. Alternatively, you might set the speed of the animation very slow and use it as a slide show to present a series of diagrams. Animated GIFs can be set either to play once and stop on the final frame, or to loop indefinitely.

Your animated GIF software will create a file with the '.gif' extension, and you can embed it in your pages exactly as you would a picture:

```
< img src='animation.gif' >
```

One particularly unattractive use of animated GIFs is as backgrounds:

```
< body background='animation.gif' >
```

Try moving horizontal or vertical lines with this one.

Adding sound to your pages

Unless you use a Java MIDI console, sound cannot really be embedded in web pages. The only other option you have is the following:

```
< bgsound src='mysound.wav' loop='2' >
```

When placed in the <head> section of your page, it will loop 'mysound.wav' twice when the page loads. You can set 'loop' to '-1' if you want it to repeat indefinitely. Unfortunately, this only works in Internet Explorer. Also, it can make your page agonisingly slow-loading because it requires you to use a 'wav' format sound file. Like the 'bitmap' format for pictures, a 'wav' is a simple but extremely uneconomical way to store sounds in a file. If you want to experiment with this effect, however, you can record 'wav' sounds using Windows Sound Recorder, or the equivalent software for your operating system.

You can make sound files available for your visitors to download using the MP3 or RealAudio formats. MP3 is easier to use, although RealAudio is more sophisticated. Both offer means of greatly compressing sound files, just as JPEG and GIF compress picture files. We will only cover MP3 here, since RealAudio requires a little more know-how to implement, and also requires you to purchase the relevant software. You can find out more here:

RealAudio
http://www.realaudio.com

Three steps are involved in making MP3 files available to your visitors:

1. Convert your existing 'wav' file into an MP3.

2. Upload it to your web site.

3. Insert a link to it from one of your pages.

Moving to the next level ....

Fig. 46. MusicMatch is one of many MP3 players for Windows 95/98. It works much like a CD player.

Here's an example link:

< a href='mysong.mp3' > Click here < /a > to listen to my song.

Your visitor's browser will encounter 'mysong.mp3', realise it's not an HTML file, and offer to save it on their hard drive for them. They can then open it using any software that can play MP3 files, and your music will come out.

MP3 is fast becoming a standard format. Most people who browse music sites regularly will have the software installed so that the browser appears to automatically open the MP3 and play it. Going even further, most players now support 'streaming'. This means that they download part of the song, and then start playing it while downloading the rest. All of this is fairly transparent to your audience, who simply click the link and hear the sounds. To create your own MP3s, you need special software, which can be found here at the popular MP3 home site:

Fig. 47. The home page of MP3.com, the internet's most popular music consumer web site.

http://www.mp3.com

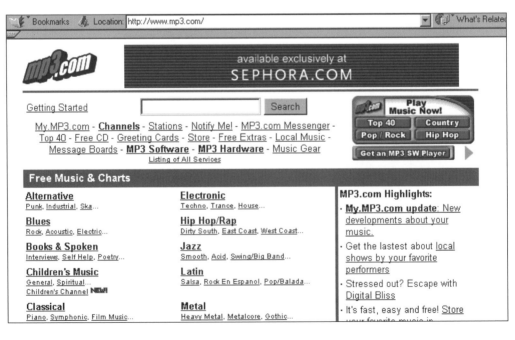

▶ *Tip* – You should only make other people's music available on your site if you have their permission to do so. Some artists will allow you to use a short excerpt for promotional purposes, but you should apply for a license from PRS/MCPS or your country's equivalent performing rights society if you want to do more than this. Always get written permission before publishing.

Other files for downloading

You can make any other kind of file available for your visitors to download, just like the MP3s. For example, if you had a Microsoft Excel spreadsheet you wanted to share with the world, you could create a link like this:

> < a href='ssheet.xls' >Download < /a> last week's gilt bond movements.

Since the browser detects that the file at the end of the hyperlink isn't a web page, it offers to either open it (or try to) or save it on the hard drive. This puts your readers in the driving seat. It makes your site more interactive, since visitors can choose which information they want to spend time downloading and which they don't.

You will quite commonly see all these types of file available for download on the web:

▶ *Software* – If you do post up software on your site, make sure you are not breaching copyright. Most freeware and shareware comes with a file explaining what you can and cannot do with it.

▶ *Customisation* – Fonts, Windows 'schemes' and other items for customising your computer. Again, some are freeware or shareware items and should be accompanied by an explanatory file.

▶ *PDF files* – If you want to post up a word-processed file but protect it from being changed, you might consider Adobe's PDF (Portable Document Format). At the time of writing this is becoming established as a standard. PDF files are also generally smaller than those created by word-processing packages, especially if they have embedded graphics, charts and so on. PDF readers are available free, but you have to pay for the software used for creating them.

▶ *Video* – This includes MPEG, AVI, and RealMovies. As you would expect, video files are extremely large and unlikely to be downloaded unless they are of particular interest to the reader. The process of encoding video files requires special hardware. It is only really worth looking into if you are sure it will add substantially to your site's value.

Any file which you are legally entitled to publish can be placed at the end of a hyperlink in this way, and downloaded by your readers. It's good practice to say how large the file is (in kb or Mb) to give people some idea of how long the download is likely to be.

Creating image maps

Image maps are another flashy feature of HTML which is easy to get wrong. They work by defining areas of a single image which can act as hyperlinks. For example, you might have a map of Europe, with each country acting as a hyperlink to information about traditional recipes from that region.

Complex image maps like the one just mentioned are very hard to do manually. It is a good idea to get a piece of software to help you. Here are a couple of good ones:

Coffee Cup
http://www.coffeecup.com/mapper/

Spinel
http://www.spinel.com/

The company has an image mapper called Web Mapper. They say: 'If you can click on a mouse, then you can make professional image maps in half the time it takes you to read this page. Download it now and give it a try.'

Fig. 48. Image-mapping with a product called Web Mapper, from Spinel.

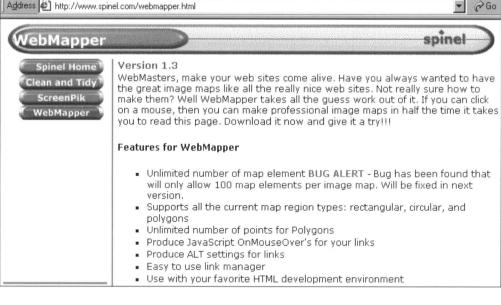

Here's an example of a simple image map. It is the sort you could create without any extra software to help you:

```
<p>
<map name='imap1'>
<area shape='polygon' coords='0, 75, 100, 0, 0, 0' href='previous' />
<area shape='polygon' coords='100, 0, 0, 75, 100%, 75' href='next' />
</map>
<img src='diagram.gif' width='100' height='75' usemap='#imap1' />
</p>
```

There are two separate things here: a description of the image map, which is between the <map> tags, and an <img/> tag with a new parameter, 'usemap'. Let's look at these one step at a time.

1. The code between the <map> tags defines an image map which is called 'imap1' (you can give it any name you like). This code could appear anywhere on the web page, even in the <head> section. This is a good place to put it because it keeps it out of the way. The image map consists of two 'polygons' which, as you may remember from school maths lessons, are any shapes with at least three sides.

2. Now, each polygon is defined with a string of co-ordinates. It uses these co-ordinates to draw the shape of each 'hot spot' on the image. These co-ordinates go in pairs. You will see that each polygon has three pairs of co-ordinates, which makes three corners. The image map will simply draw straight lines between each of these corners, in order.

3. We know that the image we want to use is 100 pixels wide by 75 pixels high. The first polygon starts in the top left-hand corner of the image – 0 pixels to the right, and 75 pixels up. It then draws a straight line to the bottom right – 100 pixels across and 0 pixels up. Next it draws a line back to the bottom left (0 pixels across and 0 pixels up). Finally, it completes the shape by joining this last point up with the first one we specified. This creates a triangular hotspot on our image; the second polygon creates a complementary triangle above this one.

4. Notice that the image map is defined quite separately from the <img/> tag, which means that several images can use the same map, as long as they are the same size and you want them divided up in the same way.

Some helpful tips
Some simple ways to avoid grief when dealing with image maps:

(a) Always provide alternate means of navigating your site, for people with browsers that don't support image maps.

(b) Design your graphics with image-mapping in mind. Don't try to force an image map onto an image which was not designed for the purpose, unless you really have to.

(c) You can draw complex image maps on graph paper to help you determine the co-ordinates if you don't want to use special software.

Don't be tempted to make your index page just an image map of your logo. This blocks many of the automated indexing processes which can benefit your site. It looks pretty unprofessional, too.

Moving to the next level ....

The future of web authoring

Anyone who claims to know what the future of the internet is going to be is clearly taking you for a ride. Here, however, are some new concepts which might or might not supplement or partially replace HTML in the next few years:

XHTML

At the time of writing, XHTML is the W3C's recommendation for a new HTML standard. That is, HTML will formally no longer exist, and will be replaced by something called XHTML. This hasn't happened yet, but by the time this book is published it may have.

XHTML is HTML, but a bit stricter. It will probably have some new bells and whistles, but the main change is that sloppy coding will not be tolerated as much as it is today. Take this piece of code, for example:

<b> This is the best site <i> in the world < /b> < /i>

Today's browsers will accept this, although it's not brilliantly logical. Future XHTML browsers may reject it, and only accept its more logical variant:

< b> This is the best site <i> in the world < /i> < /b>

Keep an eye on the web site of the World Wide Web Consortium (W3C) for the new specification. XHTML is nothing to worry about. The practice outlined in this book is XHTML-compliant, so far as one can tell at this stage, and changes will probably be minor. Also, browser makers will continue to support HTML version 4.0, which is what you have learned here. To find out more, check out the following:

Web Developers Virtual Library
http://www.wdvl.com/Authoring/Languages/XML/XHTML/

The World Wide Web Consortium
http://www.w3c.org
Keep an eye on this authoritative web site as well.

XML

XML sounds cool, and it is cool, because it is elegant and extremely flexible. XML stands for eXtensible Markup Language. In essence, it is a way of defining your own version of HTML, with tags which you have designed yourself.

Currently, XML can only be viewed using special browsers. Writing XML is quite hard, and only really suited to specialist applications. With the advent of XHTML, those things are likely to change. Smart web developers who would like to have a future in the business would be well advised to get a handle on XML, which may well be the backbone of the internet of the future – or it might be another VRML, the virtual reality modelling language which creates three-dimensional web pages.

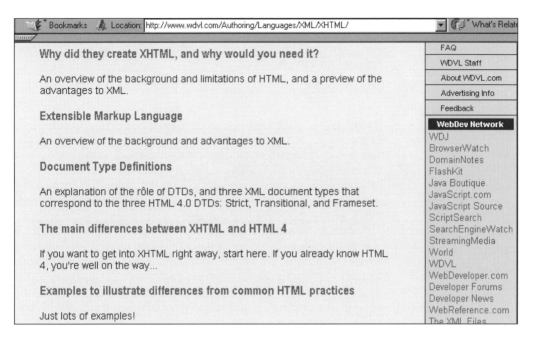

Fig. 49. The Web Developers Virtual Library contains lots of help, news and support about XHTML.

It's slow, ugly and extremely difficult to program, and it never caught on. Check out the following web pages, and make up your own mind:

http://www.xmlephant.com/

http://www.finetuning.com/

HTA

We have recently seen the advent of so-called Dynamic HTML, or DHTML. This is the result of combining HTML with Javascript and a few other new-ish technologies. Using this, programmers have started to develop real applications using browser-based code. Think about it: if you can take information from the user (with forms and 'events'), process it (with Javascript or CGI) and then present the results to the user again (with HTML), you have the basics of a viable development platform. Microsoft has caught on to this and added a new tag, < HTA >, to Internet Explorer 5.

▶ HTA stands for HyperText Application. It makes the browser behave more like a real application window.

HTA itself may not catch on, but programmers are bound to continue using DHTML to create new applications, and something akin to HTA will probably emerge as a standard.

It may surprise you to learn that, simply by reading this book, you could have gained a valuable grounding in the skills needed to work as a well-paid commercial software designer, in what may be the future employment market in that sector. Visit Microsoft to keep an eye on developments in this area if it interests you:

http://www.microsoft.com

You might like to see how often development jobs are asking for web skills, too, at a site like this:

http://www.itconnections.co.uk

Portability
At the time of writing, portability is the big buzzword on the web. The idea is that browsers running on personal computers are clunky and uneconomical. Nobody wants to fire up the PC and then wait a couple of minutes for it to boot up and dial the internet connection just to find a recipe for jam. But maybe they would look for that information using their mobile phone, their TV or their microwave.

Portability means writing pages and making them available in such a way that they look cool in any of these situations (or whichever ones are relevant, if and when this kind of internet usage becomes commonplace). The best approach is always going to be to write simple, elegantly coded pages which conform to a standard set of specifications. Watch the W3C site and other industry pages to see what emerges in this area, if anything.

Next week, of course, the buzzword might be something else.

More Internet Handbooks to help you

Brendan Murphy, *Building a Web Site on the Internet*
Kye Valongo, *Where to Find It on the Internet* (2nd edition)

Visit the free Internet HelpZone at
www.internet-handbooks.co.uk
Helping you master the internet

---

9 Finding out more online

In this chapter we will explore:

▶ *HTML tutorials*
▶ *formal HTML specifications*
▶ *cascading style sheets*
▶ *forms*
▶ *free software downloads*
▶ *learning JavaScript online*
▶ *the future of web authoring*

. . . .

It is often said that the best way to learn about the internet is by using the internet. There are lots of web sites about making web sites, although most are better suited to someone who already has an understanding of the basics. Here are some which this writer has found most useful over the years. You will, no doubt, discover gems of your own. Remember to bookmark the ones you find useful.

HTML tutorials

Both these excellent sites provide tutorials suitable for intermediate or advanced web developers; this includes you, assuming you have thoroughly read this book and not just skipped to the end.

HTML Goodies
http://www.htmlgoodies.com

Fig. 50. Web Monkey is an excellent and established source of tutorials and support, suitable for both intermediate and advanced web developers.

Finding out more online...

Web Monkey
http://www.webmonkey.com

Formal HTML specifications

The HTML described in this book will work with pretty much any combination of browsers, operating systems and software your users might have. As your site becomes more complicated, however, you will start to notice the differences more often. To help you write code which works for all your audience, the following sites are indispensable:

World Wide Web Consortium
http://www.w3c.org
The World Wide Web Consortium (W3C) exists to create standards which, if only everyone would stick to them, would ensure we were all speaking the same language. It's worth downloading a copy of their specifications for HTML 4.0 (on which this book is based), and their future recommendations, to your hard drive for easy access. The site is rather bureaucratic and confusing at first, but the content is essential reading for the intermediate to advanced web page designer.

Internet Explorer
http://developer.microsoft.com
Microsoft produces Internet Explorer, currently the world's most popular browser. It supports HTML written to the W3C standards, but it can do a lot more, too. Here you will find information about the many 'Explorer extensions' which make writing for an Explorer-only user base so much fun. Remember, however, that many of your users will not be running Explorer, but Netscape or some other browser. Make sure you test your pages in various browsers before you publish them.

Netscape Navigator
http://www.netscape.com
The same advice goes for the Netscape extensions, which are detailed on their page. At the time of writing, Netscape Navigator is the world's second most popular browser, a fact that you should take fully into account. Navigator has its own features, which you can read about here.

Cascading style sheets

Cascading style sheets (CSS) represent one part of W3C's HTML 4.0 specification not covered in this book. (Actually, a couple of style sheet tricks are included.) They aren't difficult to use, and offer a lot of powerful new features. At the time of writing the differences in implementation for Microsoft and Netscape browsers make exploiting that power rather tricky.

Having said that, CSS is definitely the wave of the future. It aims to replace the formatting tags we saw in Chapter 1 of this book with elegant structures which can even be stored in separate files, outside the HTML page. In short, style sheets will probably become essential in the future, so learning about them would be a worthwhile step if you fancy developing your page-making skills further.

Here are some places where you can find CSS tutorials online:

Developer
http://www.developer.com/journal/techworkshop/990217_css.html

HTML Goodies
http://htmlgoodies.earthweb.com/tutors/ie_style.html

Mortar
http://mortar.bigpic.com/docs/tutorial/howto/projects/projectcss1.html

At Geocities
http://www.geocities.com/SoHo/5599/sot/css/intro02.html

Forms

Forms are the other major aspect of HTML which this book doesn't cover. This is not because forms are complicated, but because they are not much use to you unless you can program in JavaScript or a CGI language like Perl. None of these things are rocket science, but they lie beyond the scope of an introductory volume like this one.

You may well have come across forms on web pages. They look like the dialogue boxes presented by some applications, with fields where you can fill in text, drop-down lists from which you can pick, say, the country where you live, and buttons to transmit the information. It's there that you need programming skills – to actually do something with the information the user has entered into the form, rather than just forgetting it again.

You can do powerful things with HTML forms combined with Java-Script and Perl. Unfortunately, this involves:

1. Learning JavaScript – not too painful, but not painless either.

2. Learning Perl – easy if you know JavaScript.

3. Getting a web hosting service that allows you to run programs on their server – which costs money.

If you want to learn about HTML forms, here are some places to do it:

HTML Goodies/Earthweb
http://htmlgoodies.earthweb.com/tutors/forms.html
The site says that this tutorial has been designed for Netscape-style browsers and Microsoft Internet Explorer 4.0 browsers only.

HTML Primer
http://htmlprimer.com/forms.shtml
The web site of HTML Primer offers a range of tutorials including on creating HTML forms, presented in easy, step-by-step lessons.

Finding out more online...

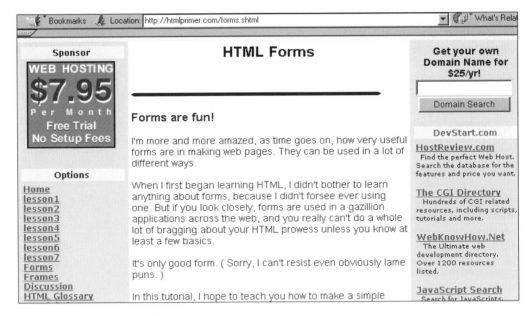

Options

Home
lesson1
lesson2
lesson3
lesson4
lesson5
lesson6
lesson7
Forms
Frames
Discussion
HTML Glossary

HTML Forms

Forms are fun!

I'm more and more amazed, as time goes on, how very useful forms are in making web pages. They can be used in a lot of different ways.

When I first began learning HTML, I didn't bother to learn anything about forms, because I didn't forsee ever using one. But if you look closely, forms are used in a gazillion applications across the web, and you really can't do a whole lot of bragging about your HTML prowess unless you know at least a few basics.

It's only good form. (Sorry, I can't resist even obviously lame puns.)

In this tutorial, I hope to teach you how to make a simple

Fig. 51. The web site of HTML Primer offers a range of tutorials including on creating HTML forms, presented in easy step-by-step lessons.

Netmar
http://info.netmar.com/creating/forms.html
Straightforward no-nonsense tutorial material on creating HTML forms.

PageTutor
http://www.pagetutor.com/pagetutor/forms/
Offers very clear and straightforward help and lessons. Free registration is required.

Web Diner
http://www.webdiner.com/annexe/forms/wdform1.htm
Free software downloads

Free software downloads

The internet being what it is, you can find almost anything you could possibly need for a web site, online and for free. Here are some well-established places to explore for:

images
music
sound effects
animations
cut-and-paste mini-programs ('scripts')
programs to embed in your pages ('applets')
stuff you didn't even know you needed yet.

City Limits
http://www.citylimits.com/software/
Contains useful lists of numerous other shareware sites. They say: 'If you have any requests for software, or are not sure where to get it, contact us and we will attempt to find it for you.'

Shareware Stockpile

http://www.stockpile.com

The site has a very useful author resources area.

Simtel

http://www.simtel.net/simtel.net

Simtel is a worldwide distribution network for shareware, freeware, and public domain software. You can explore the resources available by platform: Dos, Windows 3.x and Windows 95/98.

Software Now

http://softwarenow.iboost.com

Offers over 11,000 different software items. It provides links to freeware (software that is free and available to the general public), and shareware (you can use this software for free but if you decide to keep it then you'll be asked to pay a registration fee). There is also trial software (usually free for a specified amount of time then available after a fee has been paid), and demo software (a full or limited feature of the software that is usually free and before the full version is available).

Tucows

http://www.tucows.com

Tucows is a leading distributor of ebusiness services and applications on the internet. It works with a network of around 3,700 internet service providers, web hosting companies and domain name resellers in more than 90 countries. The site offers over 30,000 software titles in libraries located around the world, providing users with fast local downloads. The name of this hugely popular site originally derived from: 'The Ultimate Collection of Winsock Software.'

Fig. 52. Tucows offers a vast selection of useful software titles, available with fast local downloads.

Finding out more online...

UK Mirror Service
http://www.mirror.ac.uk
The UK Mirror service provides a collection of over 150 mirrors of FTP and web sites of particular interest to academia. It holds over 1,000,000 items. You can browse by subject, platform or mirror.

Learning JavaScript online

There's no doubt about it. If you've come this far, you will need to think about getting into JavaScript. It's a programming language, with all the baggage that comes with that, but it will enable you to create incredible effects which the web's creators could never have dreamed of.
Here are just some of the things you can do with JavaScript:

1.   Animate objects.

2.   Make elements in your page move.

3.   Respond to things the user does, like clicking on a button.

4.   Help your page to 'remember' users and store their preferences.

This can be astonishingly powerful. Applications that would previously have needed months of coding, only obtainable for real money, are now created in a matter of days by HTML/JavaScript programmers and made available on the web for free. Most professional sites now use some JavaScript. Indeed, some of them are entirely driven by it. Here are some online tutorials to explore, as soon as you feel ready to take the plunge:

JavaScriptGuide
http://www.javascriptguide.com
This page is for the absolute beginner to JavaScript. Some knowledge of HTML is assumed. The tips page contains some simple but useful Java-Script samples along with explanations. You can use these without knowing much about JavaScript. On the links page, you will find links to lots of JavaScript related resources on the web. The site also features a discussion forum about JavaScript and if you would like to receive email updates you can join its mailing list.

Javascript
http://www.javascript.com
This is a very helpful site that forms part of the extensive Internet.com network. You can take a detailed walk-through of a JavaScript program, and sign up for various email newsletters dealing with JavaScript and related topics.

JavaScript Search
http://www.javascriptsearch.com
Alerts, buttons, calendars, clocks, cookies, counters, forms, games, passwords – whatever you are looking for, you should be able to find it

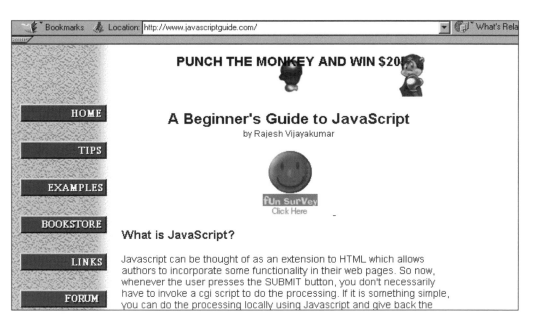

Fig. 53. The web site of
JavaScriptGuide is an
excellent starting point for
people with at least some
working knowledge of
HTML.

here. The site contains tutorials, FAQs, articles, and many other resources. JavaScriptSearch is part of the DevStart.com web developers network.

Web Developer
http://webdeveloper.com
The home page includes a link to all the tutorials offered by Web Developer. The site is part of the Internet.com network. You will find how-to instructions for everything from basic HTML to programming in Java.

Website Abstraction
http://www.wsabstract.com
The site offers scripts, JS tutorials, applets, web tutorials, a forum, and freeware java. They say: 'Over 300,000 visitors and 4 million page views monthly can't be wrong!'

More Internet Handbooks to help you

Brendan Murphy, *Building a Web Site on the Internet* (Internet Handbooks).
Kye Valongo, *Where to Find it on the Internet* (Internet Handbooks, 2nd edition).

Glossary of internet terms

access provider – The company that provides you with access to the internet. This may be an independent provider or a large international organisation such as AOL or CompuServe. See also **internet service provider**.

ActiveX – A Microsoft programming language that allows effects such as animations, games and other interactive features to be included a web page.

Adobe Acrobat – A type of software required for reading PDF files ('portable document format'). You may need to have Adobe Acrobat Reader when downloading large text files from the internet, such as lengthy reports or chapters from books. If your computer lacks it, the web page will prompt you, and usually offer you an immediate download of the free version.

address book – A directory in a web browser where you can store people's email addresses. This saves having to type them out each time you want to email someone. You just click on an address whenever you want it.

ADSL – Asymmetric Digital Subscriber Line, a new phone line technology which provides an internet connection speed up to 10 times faster than a typical modem.

affiliate programme – A system that allows you to sell other companies products via your web site.

AltaVista – One of the most popular internet search engines. Just type in a few key words to find what you want on the internet. See: www.altavista.com

AOL – America On Line, the world's biggest internet service provider, with more than 25 million subscribers, and now merged with Time Warner. It has given away vast numbers of free CDs with the popular computer magazines to build its customer base. It also owns Netscape. See: www.aol.com

Apple Macintosh – A type of computer that has its own proprietary operating system, as distinct from the MSDOS and Windows operating systems found on PCs (personal computers). The Apple Mac has long been a favourite of designers and publishers.

applet – An application programmed in Java that is designed to run only on a web browser. Applets cannot read or write data onto your computer, only from the domain in which they are served from. When a web page using an applet is accessed, the browser will download it and run it on your computer. See also **Java**.

application – Any program, such as a word processor or spreadsheet program, designed to carry out a task on your computer.

application service provider – A company that provides computer software via the internet, whereby the application is borrowed, rather than downloaded. You keep your data, they keep the program.

ARPANET – Advanced Research Projects Agency Network, an early form of the internet in the USA in the 1960s.

ASCII – American Standard Code for Information Interchange. It is a simple text file format that can be accessed by most word processors and text editors. It is a universal file type for passing textual information across the internet.

Ask Jeeves – A popular internet search engine. Rather than just typing in a few key words for your search, you can type in a whole question or instruction, such as 'Find me everything about online investment.' It draws on a database of millions of questions and answers, and works best with fairly general questions.

ASP – (1) Active Server Page, a filename extension for a type of web page. (2) Application Service Provider (see above).

attachment – A file sent with an email message. The attached file can be anything from a word-processed document to a database, spreadsheet, graphic, or even a sound or video file. For example you could email someone birthday greetings, and attach a sound track or video clip.

Authenticode – Authenticode is a system whereby ActiveX controls can be authenticated in some way, usually by a certificate.

avatar – A cartoon or image used to represent someone on screen while taking part in internet chat.

backup – A second copy of a file or a set of files. Backing up data is essential if there is any risk of data loss.

bandwidth – The width of the electronic highway that gives you access to the internet. The higher the bandwidth, the wider this highway, and the faster the traffic can flow.

banner ad – This is a band of text and graphics, usually situated at the top of a web page. It acts like a title, telling the user what the content of the page is about. It invites the visitor to click on it to visit that site. Banner advertising has become big business.

baud rate – The data transmission speed in a modem, measured in kbps (kilobits per second).

BBS – Bulletin board service. A facility to read and to post public messages at a particular web site.

binary numbers – The numbering system used by computers. It only uses 1s and 0s to represent numbers. Decimal numbers are based on the number 10. You can count from nought to nine. When you count higher than nine, the nine is replaced with a 10. Binary numbers are based on the number 2: each place can only have the value of 1 or 0.

Blue Ribbon Campaign – A widely supported campaign supporting free speech and opposing moves to censor the internet by all kinds of elected and unelected bodies. See the Electronic Frontier Foundation at: www.eff.org

bookmark – A file of URLs of your favourite internet sites. – Bookmarks are very easily created by bookmarking (mouse-clicking) any internet page you like the look of. If you are an avid user, you could soon end up with hundreds of them! In the Internet Explorer browser and AOL they are called Favorites.

Boolean search – A search in which you type in words such as AND and OR to refine your search. Such words are called 'Boolean operators'. The concept is named after George Boole, a nineteenth-century English mathematician.

bot – Short for robot. It is used to refer to a program that will perform a task on the internet, such as carrying out a search.

browser – Your browser is your window to the internet, and will normally supplied by your internet service provider when you first sign up. It is the program that you use to access the world wide web, and manage your personal communications and privacy when online. By far the two most popular browsers are Microsoft Internet Explorer and Netscape Navigator. You can easily swap, or use both. Both can be downloaded free from their web sites (a lengthy process) and are found on the CD roms stuck to the computer magazines. It won't make much difference which one you use – they both do much the same thing. Opera (www.opera.com) is an alternative, as is NetCaptor (www.netcaptor.com). – America Online (www.aol.com) has its own proprietary browser which is not available separately.

bug – A weakness in a program or a computer system. They are remedied by 'fixes' or 'patches' which can be downloaded.

bulletin board – A type of computer-based news service that provides an email service and a file archive.

cache – A file storage area on a computer. Your web browser will normally cache (copy to your hard drive) each web page you visit. When you revisit that page on the web, you may in fact be looking at the page originally cached on your computer. To be sure you are viewing the current page, press **reload** or **re-**

Add Bookmark
File Bookmark
Edit Bookmarks...

Books & publishing
Business
Collecting
Directories
Education
Entertainment
Help
Internet
Jobs and careers
News

fresh on your browser toolbar. You can empty your cache from time to time, and the computer will do so automatically whenever the cache is full. In Internet Explorer, pages are saved in the Windows folder, Temporary Internet Files. In Netscape they are saved in a folder called Cache.

certificate – A computer file that securely identifies a person or organisation on the internet.

CGI – Common gateway interface. This defines how the web server should pass information to the program, such as what it's being asked to do, what objects it should work with, any inputs, and so on.

channel (chat) – Place where you can chat with other internet chatters. The name of a chat channel is prefixed with a hash mark, #.

clickstream – The sequence of hyperlinks clicked by someone when using the internet.

click through – This is when someone clicks on a banner ad or other link, for example, and is moved from that page to the advertiser's web site.

client – This is the term given to any program that you use to access the internet. For example your web browser is a web client, your email program is an email client, your newsreader is a news client, and your chat software is a chat client.

community – The internet is often described as a community. This refers to the fact that many people like the feeling of belonging to a group of like-minded individuals. Many big web sites have been developed along these lines, such as GeoCities (www.geocities.com) which is divided into special-interest neighbourhoods, or America Online (www.aol.com) which is strong on member services.

compression – Computer files can be electronically compressed, so that they can be uploaded or downloaded more quickly across the internet, saving time and money. With some forms of compression, there may be a loss of quality. To read them, you uncompress them.

configure – To set up, or adjust the settings of, a computer or software program.

content – The articles, messages, forums, images, text, hyperlinks and other features of a web site.

cookie – A cookie is a small code that the server asks your browser to keep until it asks for it. If it sends it with the first page and asks for it back before each other page, they can follow you around the site, even if you switch your computer off in between.

cracker – Someone who breaks into computer systems with the intention of causing some kind of damage or system abuse.

crash – What happens when a computer program malfunctions. The operating system of your PC may perform incorrectly or come to a complete stop ('freeze'), forcing you to shut down and restart.

cross-posting – Posting an identical message in several different newsgroups or mailing lists at the same time.

cybercash – This is a trademark, but is also often used as a broad term to describe the use of small payments made over the internet using a new form of electronic account that is loaded up with cash. You can send this money to the companies offering such cash facilities by cheque, or by credit card. Some internet companies offering travel-related items can accept electronic cash of this kind.

cyberspace – Popular term for the intangible 'place' where you go to surf – the ethereal world of computers and telecommunications on the internet.

cypherpunk remailer – Cypherpunk remailers strip headers from the messages and add new ones.

cybersquatting – Using someone else's name or trademark as your domain name in the hope they will buy it from you.

data – Pieces of information (singular: datum). Data can exist in many forms such

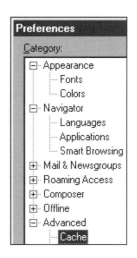

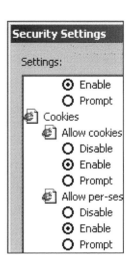

as numbers in a spreadsheet, text in a document, or as binary numbers stored in a computer's memory.

database – A store of information in digital form. Many web sites make use of substantial databases to deliver maximum content at high speed to the web user.

dial-up account – This allows you to connect your (local) computer to your internet service provider's (remote) computer.

digital – Based on the two binary digits, 1 and 0. The operation of all computers is based on this amazingly simple concept. All forms of information are capable of being digitised – numbers, words, and even sounds and images – and then transmitted over the internet.

digital signature – A unique and secure personal signature specially created for use over the internet. It is designed to fulfil a similar function to that of the traditional handwritten signature.

directory – On a PC, a folder containing your files.

DNS – Domain name server.

domain name – A name that identifies an IP address. It identifies to the computers on the rest of the internet where to access particular information. Each domain has a name. For someone@somewhere.co.uk, 'somewhere' is the domain name.

download – Downloading means copying a file from one computer on the internet to your own computer. You do this by clicking on a button that links you to the appropriate file. Downloading is an automatic process, except that you have to click 'yes' to accept the download and give it a file name. You can download any type of file – text, graphics, sound, spreadsheet, computer programs, and so on.

ebusiness – The broad concept of doing business to business, and business to consumer sales, over the internet.

ecash – Short for electronic cash. See **cybercash.**

ecommerce – The various means and techniques of transacting business online.

email – Electronic mail, any message or file you send from your computer to another computer using your email client program (such as Netscape Messenger or Microsoft Outlook).

email address – The unique address given to you by your ISP. It can be used by others using the internet to send email messages to you. An email address always has at 'at' sign in the middle, for example:

myname@myISP.com

email bomb – An attack by email in which the victim is sent hundreds or thousands of email messages in a very short period of time. Such an attack could prevent you from receiving genuine email messages.

emoticons – Popular symbols used to express emotions in email, for example the well-known smiley :-) which means 'don't take this too seriously.' Emoticons are not normally appropriate for business communications.

encryption – The scrambling of information to make it unreadable without a key or password. Email and any other data can now be encrypted using PGP and other freely available programs. Modern encryption has become so amazingly powerful as to be to all intents and purposes uncrackable.

Excite – A popular internet directory and search engine used to find pages relating to specific keywords which you enter. See: www.excite.com

ezines – The term for magazines and newsletters published on the internet.

FAQs – Frequently asked questions. You will see 'FAQ' everywhere you go on the internet. If you are ever doubtful about anything check the FAQ page, if the site has one, and you should find the answers to your queries.

favorites – The rather coy term for **bookmarks** used by Internet Explorer, and by America Online. Maintaining a list of Favorites is designed to make

Dial-Up Networking

Get Excite

Message Centre

✉ **Your Free Email**

· **Free Voicemail/Fax**

Featured Today

✗ **NEWS:** British barricade at N.Irish hotspot

Poll: Summer Film Favour New! Top Mp3 Downloads [Chat & Make Friends]

returning to web sites easier, by saving their addresses.

file – A file is any body of data such as a word processed document, a spreadsheet, a database file, a graphics or video file, sound file, or computer program. On a PC, every file has a filename, and a filename extension showing what type of file it is.

filtering software – Software loaded onto a computer to prevent access by someone to unwelcome content on the internet. The well-known 'parental controls' include CyberSitter, CyberPatrol, SurfWatch and NetNanny. They can be blunt instruments. For example, if they are programmed to reject all web pages containing the word 'virgin', you would not be able to access any web page hosted at Richard Branson's Virgin Net. Of course, there are also web sites that tell you step-by-step how to disable or bypass these filtering tools.

finger – A tool for locating people on the internet. The most common use is to see if a person has an account at a particular internet site. It also means a chat command that returns information about the other chat user, including idle time (time since they last did anything).

firewall – A firewall is special security software designed to stop the flow of certain files into and out of a computer network, e.g. viruses or attacks by hackers. A firewall would be an important feature of any fully commercial web site.

flame – A more or less hostile or aggressive message posted in a newsgroup or to an individual newsgroup user.

folder – The name for a directory on a computer. It is a place in which files are stored.

form – A web page that allows or requires you to enter information into fields on the page and send the information to a web site, program or individual on the web. Forms are often used for registration or sending questions and comments to web sites.

forums – Places for discussion on the internet. They include Usenet newsgroups, mailing lists, and bulletin board services.

frames – A web design feature in which web pages are divided into several areas or panels, each containing separate information. A typical set of frames in a page includes an index frame (with navigation links), a banner frame (for a heading), and a body frame (for text matter).

freespace – An allocation of free web space by an internet service provider or other organisation, to its users or subscribers, typically between 5 and 20 megabytes.

freeware – Software programs made available without charge. Where a small charge is requested, the term is **shareware**.

front page – The first page of your web site that the visitor will see. FrontPage is also the name of a popular web authoring package from Microsoft.

FTP – File transfer protocol, the method the internet uses to speed files back and forth between computers. Your browser will automatically select this method, for instance, when you want to download your bank statements to reconcile your accounts. In practice you don't need to worry about FTP unless you are thinking about creating and publishing your own web pages: then you would need some of the freely available FTP software. Despite the name, it's easy to use.

GIF – Graphic interchange format. It is a widely-used compressed file format used on web pages and elsewhere to display files that contain graphic images. See also **JPEG** and **MPEG**.

GUI – Short for graphical user interface. It describes the user-friendly screens found in Windows and other WIMP environments (windows, icons, mice, pointers).

hacker – A person interested in computer programming, operating systems, the

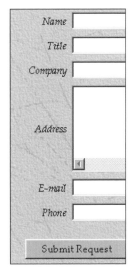

internet and computer security. The term can be used to describe a person who breaks into computer systems with the intention of pointing out the weaknesses in a system. In common usage, the term is often wrongly used to describe crackers.

header – That part of an email message or newsgroup posting which contains information about the sender and the route that the message took across the internet.

history list – A record of visited web pages. Your browser probably includes a history list. It is handy way of revisiting sites whose addresses you have forgotten to bookmark – just click on the item you want in the history list. You can normally delete all or part of the history list in your browser.

hit counter – A piece of software used by a web site to record the number of hits it has received.

hits – The number of times pieces of text, images, hyperlinks and other components of a web page have been viewed. A better measure of a site's popularity would be the number of page views, or the number of user sessions.

home page – This refers to the index page of an individual or an organisation on the internet. It usually contains links to related pages of information, and to other relevant sites.

host – A host is the computer where a particular file or domain is located, and from where people can retrieve it.

HotBot – A popular internet search engine used to find pages relating to any keywords you decide to enter.

HTML – Hypertext markup language, the universal computer language used to create pages on the world wide web. It is much like word processing, but uses special 'tags' to format the text and create hyperlinks to other web pages.

HTTP – Hypertext transfer protocol, the protocol used by the world wide web. It is the language spoken between your browser and the web servers. It is the standard way in which HTML documents are transferred from host computers to your local browser when you're surfing the internet. You'll see this acronym at the start of every web address, for example:

http://www.abcxyz.com

With modern browsers, it is no longer necessary to enter 'http://' at the start of the address.

hyperlink – See **link**.

hypertext – Text containing links which, when clicked with a mouse, result in a further HTML page or graphic being loaded into view on your browser.

IANA – The Internet Assigned Numbers Authority, the official body responsible for ensuring that the numerical coding of the internet works properly.

ICANN – The committee that oversees the whole domain name system.

ICQ – A form of internet chat, derived from the phrase 'I seek you'. It enables users to be alerted whenever fellow users go online, so they can have instant chat communication.

impression – An internet advertising term that means the showing of a single instance of an advert on a single computer screen.

Infoseek – One of the ten most popular internet search engines, now teamed up with Disney in the GO Network.

Intel – Manufacturer of the Pentium and Celeron microprocessors.

internet – The broad term for the expanding network of global computers that can access each other in seconds by phone and satellite links. If you are using a modem on your computer, you too are part of the internet. The general term 'internet' encompasses email, the world wide web, internet chat, Usenet newsgroups, mailing lists, bulletin boards, telnet, and video conferencing. It is rather like the way we speak of 'the printed word' when we mean books, magazines, newspapers, newsletters, catalogues, leaflets, tickets and posters. The 'internet' does not exist in one place any more than 'the printed word' does.

Internet2 – A new form of the internet being developed exclusively for educational and academic use.

internet account – The account set up by your internet service provider which gives you access to the world wide web, electronic mail facilities, newsgroups and other services.

internet directory – A special web site which consists of information about other sites. The information is classified by subject area and further subdivided into smaller categories. The biggest and most widely used is Yahoo! – www.yahoo.com. See also **search engines**.

Internet Explorer – The world's most popular browser software, a product of Microsoft and leading the field against Netscape.

internet protocol number – The numerical code that is a web site's real domain name address, rather than its alphabetical name.

internet service providers – ISPs are commercial, educational or official organisations which offer people ('users') access to the internet. The well-known commercial ones include AOL, CompuServe, BT Internet, Freeserve, Demon and Virgin Net. Services typically include access to the world wide web, email and newsgroups, as well as others such as news, chat, and entertainment.

intranet – Software that allows communication between individuals, for example within a large commercial organisation. It often operates on a LAN (local area network).

IP address – An 'internet protocol' address. The address is somewhat like a telephone number, and consists of four sets of numbers separated by dots.

IPv6 – The new internet coding system that will allow even more domain names.

IRC – Internet relay chat. Chat is an enormously popular part of the internet, and there are all kinds of chat rooms and chat software. Chat involves typing messages which are sent and read in real time. It was developed in 1988 by Jarkko Oikarinen.

ISDN – Integrated Services Digital Network. This is a telephone network that can send computer data from the internet to your PC faster than a normal telephone line.

Java – A programming language developed by Sun Microsystems to use the special properties of the internet to create graphics and multimedia applications on web sites.

JavaScript – A programming language that can be put onto a web page to create interactive effects such as buttons that change appearance when you position the mouse over them.

JPEG – The acronym is short for Joint Photographic Experts Group. A JPEG is a specialised file format used to display graphic files on the internet. JPEG files can be smaller than similar GIF files and so have become ever more popular – even though their quality is not as good as GIF format files. See also MPEG.

key shortcut – Two keys pressed at the same time. Usually the Control key (Ctrl), Alt key, or Shift key combined with a letter or number. For example, to use Control-D, press Control, tap the D key once firmly, then take your finger off the Control key.

keywords – Words that sum up your web site for search engines indexes. For example for a cosmetic site the keywords might include beauty, lipstick, make-up, fashion, cosmetic and so on.

kick – To eject someone from a chat channel.

LAN – A local area network, a computer network usually located in one building or campus.

link – A hypertext phrase or image that calls up another web page when you click

on it. Most web sites have lots of hyperlinks – links for short. These appear on the screen as buttons, images or bits of text (often underlined) that you can click on with your mouse to jump to another site on the world wide web.

Linux – A new widely and freely available operating system for personal computers, and a potentially serious challenger to Microsoft. It has developed a considerable following.

LINX – The London Internet Exchange, the facility which maintains UK internet traffic in the UK. It allows existing individual internet service providers to exchange traffic within the UK, and improve connectivity and service for their customers. LINX is one of the largest and fastest growing exchange points in Europe, and maintains connectivity between the UK and the rest of the world.

listserver – An automated email system whereby subscribers are able to receive and send email from other subscribers to the same mailing list. See: www.liszt.com

log on/log off – To access/leave a network. In the early days of computing this literally involved writing a record in a log book. You may be asked to 'log on' to certain sites and particular pages. This normally means entering your user ID in the form of a name and a password.

lurk – The term used to describe reading the messages in a newsgroup without actually posting messages yourself.

macros – 'Macro languages' are used to automate repetitive tasks in Word processors and other applications. They can carry viruses.

mail server – A remote computer that enables you to send and receive emails. Your internet access provider will usually act as your mail server, storing your incoming messages until you go online to retrieve them.

mailing list – A forum where messages are distributed by email to the members of the forum. The two types of lists are discussion and announcement. Discussion lists allow exchange between list members. Announcement lists are one-way only and used to distribute information such as news or humour. A good place to find mailing lists is Liszt : www.liszt.com

marquee – A moving (scrolling) line of text on a web site.

Media player – Windows software on a personal computer that will play sounds and images including video clips and animations.

metasearch engine – A site that sends a keyword search to many different search engines and directories so you can use many search engines from one place.

meta tags The technical term for the keywords used in web page code to help search engine software rank the site.

Microsoft – A major producer of software for personal computers, including the Windows operating systems, and the web browser Internet Explorer.

Mixmaster – An anonymous remailer that sends and receives email messages as packages of exactly the same size and often randomly varies the delay time between receiving and remailing to make interception harder.

modem – This is an internal or external piece of hardware plugged into your PC. It links into a standard phone socket, thereby giving you access to the internet. The word derives from MOdulator and DEModulator.

moderator – A person in charge of a mailing list, newsgroup or forum. The moderator prevents unwanted messages from reaching the list's members.

MPEG or MPG – The file format used for video clips available on the internet. See also JPEG.

MP3 – An immensely popular audio format that allows you to download and play music on your computer. It compresses music to create files that are small yet whose quality is almost as good as CD music. At the time of writing, MP4, even faster to download was being developed. See the consumer web site: www.mp3.com

MUDs – Multi-user dungeons, interactive chat-based fantasy world games. Popular in the early days of the internet, they are now in decline with the advance of networked arcade games such as Quake and Unreal.

navigate – To click on the hyperlinks on a web site in order to move to other web pages or internet sites.

net – A term for the internet. In the same way, the world wide web is often just called the web.

netiquette – Popular term for the unofficial rules and language people follow to keep electronic communication in an acceptably polite form.

Netmeeting – This Microsoft plug in allows a moving video picture to be contained within a web page. It is now integrated into Windows Media Player.

Netscape – After Microsoft's Internet Explorer, Netscape Navigator is the most popular browser software available for surfing the internet. Netscape Communicator comes complete with email, newsgroups, address book and bookmarks, plus a web page composer. Netscape is now part of American Online.

newbie – Popular term for a new member of a newsgroup or mailing list.

newsgroup – A Usenet discussion group. Each newsgroup is a collection of messages, usually unedited and not checked by anyone ('unmoderated'). Anyone can post messages to a newsgroup. It is rather like reading and sending public emails. The ever-growing newsgroups have been around for much longer than the world wide web, and are an endless source of information, gossip, news, entertainment, sex, scandal, politics, resources and ideas. The 80,000-plus newsgroups are collectively referred to as Usenet, and millions of people use it every day.

newsreader – A type of software that enables you to search, read, post and manage messages in a newsgroup. It will normally be supplied by your internet service provider when you first sign up, or preloaded on your new computer. The best known newsreaders are Microsoft Outlook and Netscape Messenger.

news server – A remote computer (e.g. your internet service provider) that enables you to access newsgroups. If you cannot get some or any newsgroups from your existing news server, use your favourite search engine to search for 'open news servers' – there are lots available.

nick – Nickname, an alias you can give yourself and use when entering a chat channel, rather than using your real name.

Nominet – The official body for registering domain names in the UK, for example web sites whose name ends in .co.uk.

Notepad – The most basic type of word processor that comes with a Windows PC. To find it, click Start, Programs, then Accessories. Its very simplicity makes it ideal for writing and saving HTML pages.

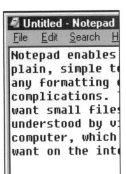

online – The time you spend linked via a modem to the internet. You can keep your phone bill down by reducing online time. The opposite term is offline.

open source software – A type of freely modifiable software, such as Linux. A definition and more information can be found at: www.opensource.org

OS – The operating system in a computer, for example MS DOS (Microsoft Disk Operating System), or Windows 95/98/2000.

packet – The term for any small piece of data sent or received over the internet on your behalf by your internet service provider. It contains your address and the recipient's address. One email message for example may be transmitted as several different packets of information, and reassembled at the other end to recreate the message. The contents of packets can be detected by sniffer software, as used for example by ISPs.

parking – Placing a web domain into storage until it is wanted for public use at a later date.

Passwords

password – A word or series of letters and numbers that enables a user to access a file, computer or program. A passphrase is a password made by using more than one word.

patch – A small piece of software used to patch up a hole or defect ('bug') in a software program.

PC – Personal computer, based on IBM technology. It is distinct from the Apple Macintosh which uses its own different operating system.

PDA – Personal data assistant, a mobile phone, palm top or any other hand-held processor, typically used to access the internet.

PDF – Portable document format, a handy type of file produced using Adobe Acrobat software. It has wide applications for text and graphics.

Pentium – The name of a very popular microprocessor chip used in personal computers, manufactured by Intel.

PGP – Pretty Good Privacy. A proprietary and free method of encoding a message before transmitting it over the internet. With PGP, a message is first compressed then encoded with the help of a pair of keys. Just like the valuables in a locked safe, your message is safe unless a person has access to the right keys. Many governments now want complete access to people's private keys. See: www.pgpi.com

ping – A ping test is used to check the connection speed between one computer and another.

plugin – A type of (usually free and downloadable) software required to add some form of functionality to web page viewing. A well-known example is Macromedia Shockwave, a plugin that enables you to view animations.

PoP – Point of presence. This refers to the dial-up phone numbers available from your ISP. If your ISP does not have a local point of presence (i.e. local access phone number), then don't sign up – your telephone bill will rocket because you will be charged national phone rates. All the major ISPs have local numbers covering the whole of the country.

portal site – Portal means gateway. It is a web site designed to be used as a base from which to explore the internet, or some particular part of it. Yahoo! is a good example of a portal (www.yahoo.com). A portal site includes the one that loads into your browser each time you connect to the internet. It could for example be the front page of your internet service provider.

post – The common term used for sending ('posting') messages ('articles') to a newsgroup. Posting messages is very like sending emails, except of course that they are public and everyone can read them. Also, newsgroup postings are archived, and can be read by anyone in the world years later. Because of this, many people feel more comfortable using an 'alias' (made-up name) when posting messages. See: www.deja.com

privacy – Unless you take steps to protect yourself, you have practically no personal privacy online. To explore privacy issues worldwide visit the authoritative Electronic Frontier Foundation web site: www.eff.org. For the UK see: www.netfreedom.org

program – A series of coded instructions designed to automatically control a computer in carrying out a specific task. Programs are written in special languages including Java, JavaScript, VBScript, and ActiveX.

protocol – On the internet, a protocol means a set of technical rules that has been agreed and is used between participating systems. For example, for viewing web pages your computer would use hypertext transfer protocol (http). For downloading and uploading files, it would use file transfer protocol (ftp).

proxy – An intermediate computer or server, used for reasons of security.

Quicktime – A popular free software program from Apple Computers. It is designed to play sounds and images including video clips and animations on both Apple Macs and personal computers.

radio button – A button which, when clicked, looks like this: ⊙

refresh, reload – The refresh or reload button on your browser toolbar tells the web page you are looking at to reload.

register – You may have to give your name, personal details and financial information to some sites before you can continue to use the pages. Site owners may want to produce a mailing list to offer you products and services. Registration is also used to discourage casual traffic. A high proportion of internet users enter fictional details to protect their privacy.

registered user – Someone who has filled out an online form and then been granted permission to access a restricted area of a web site. Access is usually obtained by logging on, typically by entering a password and user name.

remailer – A remailer is an internet service that preserves your privacy by acting as a go-between when you browse or send email messages. An anonymous remailer is simply a computer connected to the internet that can forward an email message to other people after stripping off the header of the messages. Once a message is routed through an anonymous remailer, the recipient of that message, or anyone intercepting it, can no longer identify its origin.

RFC – Request for comment. RFCs are used by the internet developers as a method of proposing changes and discussing standards and procedures. See: http://rs.internic.net

RSA – One of the most popular methods of encryption, and used in Netscape browsers. See: www.rsa.com

router – A machine that directs all internet data (packets) from one internet location to another.

rules – The term for message filters in Outlook Express.

script – A script is a set of commands written into the HTML tags of a web page. Script languages such as JavaScript and VBScript work in a similar way to macros in a word processor. Scripts are hidden from view but are executed when you open a page or click a link containing script instructions.

scroll, scroll bar – To scroll means to move part of a page or document into view, or out of view, on the screen. Scrolling is done by using a scroll bar activated by the mouse pointer. Grey scroll bars automatically appear on the right and/or lower edge of the screen if the page contents are too big to fit into view.

search engine – A search engine is a web site you can use for finding something on the internet. The information-gathering technology variously involves the use of 'bots' (search robots), spiders or crawlers. Popular search engines and internet directories have developed into big web sites and information centres in their own right. There are hundreds of them. Among the best known are AltaVista, Excite, Google, Infoseek, Lycos, Metasearch, Webcrawler and Yahoo!.

secure servers – The hardware and software provided so that people can use their credit cards and leave other details without the risk of others seeing them online. Your browser will flash up a reassuring notice when you are entering and leaving a secure site.

secure sockets layer (SSL) – A standard piece of technology which ensures secure financial transactions and data flow over the internet.

security certificate – Information that is used by the SSL protocol to establish a secure connection. Security certificates contain information about who it belongs to, who it was issued by, some form of unique identification, valid dates, and an encrypted fingerprint that can be used to verify the contents of the certificate.

server – Any computer on a network that provides access and serves information to other computers.

shareware – Software that you can try before you buy. Usually there is some kind of limitation such as an expiry date. To get the registered version, you must pay for the software, typically $20 to $40. A vast amount of shareware is now available online.

Shockwave – A popular piece of software produced by Macromedia, which enables you to view animations and other special effects on web sites. You can download this plugin for free, and in a few minutes, from Macromedia's web site. The effects can be fun, but they slow down the speed at which the pages load into your browser window. See: www.macromedia.com

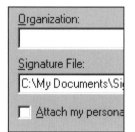

signature file – This is a little text file in which you can place your address details, for adding to email and newsgroup messages. Once you have created a signature file, it is automatically appended to your emails. You can of course delete or edit it at any time.

Slashdot – A leading technology news web site. See: http://slashdot.org

smiley – A form of **emoticon**.

snail mail – The popular term for the standard postal service involving post-persons, vans, trains, planes, sacks and sorting offices.

sniffer – A program on a computer system (usually an ISP's system) designed to collect information. Sniffers may be used by hackers to harvest passwords and user names, and by surveillance agencies to target wrongdoers.

spam – The popular term for electronic junk mail – unsolicited and unwelcome email messages sent across the internet. There are various forms of spam-busting software which can filter out unwanted email messages.

SSL – Secure socket layer, a key part of internet security technology.

subscribe – The term for accessing a newsgroup in order to read and post messages in the newsgroup. There is no charge, and you can subscribe, unsubscribe and resubscribe at will with a click of your mouse. Unless you post a message, no one in the newsgroup will know that you have subscribed or unsubscribed.

surfing – Slang term for browsing the internet, especially following trails of links on pages across the world wide web.

sysop – Systems operator, someone rather like a moderator, for example, of a chat room or bulletin board service.

talkers – Chat servers which give users the opportunity to talk to each other. You connect to them, take a 'nickname' and start chatting. Usually, they offer some other features besides just allowing users to talk to each other, including bulletin boards, a virtual world such as a city or building, which you move around in, an opportunity to store some information on yourself, and some games.

TCP/IP – Transmission control protocol/internet protocol, the essential communication rules of the internet.

telnet – Software that allows you to connect across the internet to a remote computer (e.g. a university department or library). You can then access that computer as if you were on a local terminal linked to that system.

template – A pre-designed page which you can adapt in various ways to suit your own needs. Templates are widely used, for example, in popular web authoring packages such as Microsoft Front Page Express.

theme – A term in web page design used to describe the general colours and graphics used within a web site. Many themes are available in the form of ready-made templates.

thread – An ongoing topic in a Usenet newsgroup or mailing list discussion. The term refers to the original message on a particular topic, and all the replies and other messages which spin off from it. With newsreading software, you can easily 'view thread' and thus read the related messages in a convenient batch.

thumbnail – A small version of a graphic file which, when clicked on screen, displays a larger version.

top level domain – The last element of a web site's domain name, such as .com or .uk or .net

traceroute – A program that traces the route from your machine to a remote system. It is useful if you need to discover a person's ISP, for example in the case of a spammer.

traffic – The amount of data flowing across the internet, to a particular web site, newsgroup or chat room, or as emails.

trojan horse – A program that seems to perform a useful task but which in fact disguises a malevolent program designed to cause damage to a computer system.

UNIX – This is a computer operating system that has been in use for many years, and still is used in many larger systems. Most ISPs use it.

uploading – The act of copying files from your PC to a server or other PC on the internet, for example when you are publishing your own web pages. It describes the act of copying HTML pages onto the internet via FTP.

URL – Uniform resource locator the address of each internet page. For instance the URL of Internet Handbooks is: http://www.internet-handbooks.co.uk

Usenet – The collection of well over 80,000 active newsgroups that make up a substantial part of the internet.

virtual reality – The presentation of a lifelike scenario in electronic form. It can be used for gaming, business or educational purposes.

virtual server – A portion of a PC that is used to host your own web domain (if you have one).

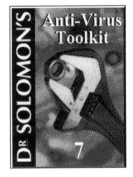

virus – A computer program maliciously designed to damage computer files. Viruses can typically be received when downloading program files from the internet, or from copying material from infected disks. Even Word files can be infected through macros. You can protect yourself from the vast majority of them by installing some inexpensive anti-virus software, such as products made by Norton, McAfee or Dr Solomon.

web authoring – Creating HTML pages to upload onto the internet. You will be a web author if you create your own home page for uploading onto the internet.

web – Short for the world wide web. See **WWW** below.

WAP – Wireless Application Protocol, technology that enables mobile phones and other portal gadgets to access the internet.

web-based chat – A form of internet chat which just uses web pages, and does not require special software like IRC and ICQ. For web-based chat, the settings in your browser must be Java-enabled. Most modern browsers are Java-enabled by default.

web client – Another term for a web browser.

Webcrawler – A popular internet search engine used to find pages relating to specific keywords entered.

webmaster – Any person who manages a web site.

web page – Any single page of information you can view on the world wide web. A typical web page includes a unique URL (address), headings, text, images, and hyperlinks (usually in the form of graphic icons, or underlined text). One web page usually contains links to lots of other web pages, either within the same web site or elsewhere on the world wide web.

web rings – A network of interlinked web sites that share a common interest. See: www.webring.org

web site – A set of web pages, owned or managed by the same person or organisation, and which are interconnected by hyperlinks.

whois – A network service that allows you to consult a database containing information about someone. A whois query can, for example, help to find the identity of someone who is sending you unwanted email messages.

Windows – The ubiquitous operating system for personal computers developed by Bill Gates and the Microsoft Corporation. The Windows 3.1 version was followed by Windows 95 and 98. Windows 2000 is the latest.

wizard – A feature of many software programs that steps you through its main stages, for example with the use of readymade templates or options.

WWW – The world wide web. Since it began in the 1990s this has become the most popular part of the internet. The web is now made up of more than a billion web pages of every imaginable description, typically linking to other pages.

WYSIWYG – 'What you see is what you get.' If you see it on the screen, then it should look just the same when you print it out.

Yahoo! – Probably the world's most popular internet directory and search engine, valued on Wall Street at billions of dollars: www.yahoo.com

zip/unzip – Many files that you download from the internet will be in compressed format, especially if they are large files. This is to make them quicker to download. Zip files have the extension '.zip' and are easily created (and unzipped) using WinZip or a similar popular software package. See: www.winzip.com

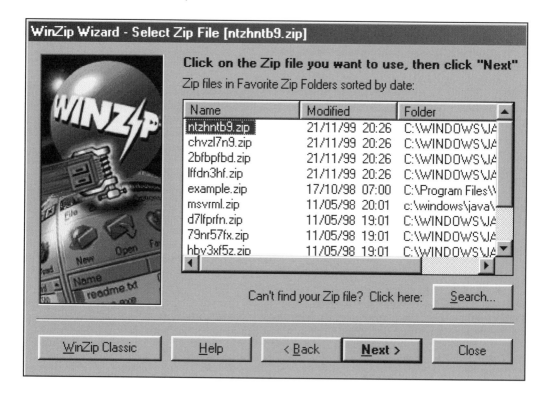

Index..

Books & Publishing on the Internet
An essential guide for authors, readers, editors, booksellers, librarians & publishing professionals
Roger Ferneyhough MA(Oxon)

Are you an author, bookseller, publisher or editor? Here is a guide to today's whole new world of books and publishing information online. The book reviews web sites of every imaginable kind – of publishers, bookstores, writers' groups, literary agents, book fairs, book distributors, training organisations, prizes, book-related associations, pressure groups, periodicals and many more. Whether you are planning to write, edit, publish or distribute a book, or want to contact a specialist, this is the book for you.
1 84025 332 0

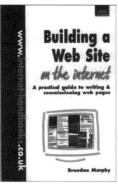

Building a Web Site on the Internet
A practical guide to writing and commissioning web pages
Brendan Murphy BSc(Hons)

This book meets the urgent need for all business users who need an effective internet presence. Written in plain English, it explains the three main ways of achieving this: create it yourself by writing HTML, create it yourself by using a popular software package, or create it by hiring a web development company. Whether your organisation is large or small, make sure *you* make the right choices for your web site. Brendan Murphy BSc MBA MBSC teaches HNC in Computing, and lectures on the internet for the Open University. He is a Member of the British Computer Society, and Institute of Management Information Systems.
1 84025 314 2

Careers Guidance on the Internet
An essential guide to careers and vocational guidance resources online
Laurel Alexander

Are you planning to apply for a new job, or seeking promotion, or looking for new skills? Perhaps you are responsible for providing careers guidance to adults or young people? Careers information – like so many other things – is being challenged and revolutionised by the internet. New internet knowledge and skills are urgently needed by every professional working in this vital field. Packed with expert advice, and concise reviews of key web sites, this timely book will help you take full advantage of some amazing new online resources. Laurel Alexander MIPD MICG is a qualified trainer, assessor and guidance specialist.
1 84025 351 7

Chat & Chat Rooms on the Internet
A practical guide to exploring the live net chat communities
Mark Ray MSc

Whether you are a recent entrant into the internet world, an experienced web user, or even a dedicated operator of an Internet Relay Chat channel, this book provides an in-depth guide to talkers and IRC. It includes detailed snapshots of real online conversations, information on the major networks, and explains how to download and use the tested client software. Written with the help of some of those who make up these new communities, it also looks at how some have organised themselves into virtual democracies, how they are developing, and discusses where all this fantastic new technology may lead. Mark Ray MSc is the webmaster and system operator for the Union of University of East Anglia Students.
1 84025 347 9

Discussion Forums on the Internet
A practical step-by-step guide to newsgroups, mailing lists and bulletin board services
Kye Valongo

A vast number of messages are posted into newsgroups, mailing lists and bulletin board services every day, and millions of people all over the world love to read them. These forums cover every imaginable subject, from local interest to jobs and travel, education, finance, entertainment, raunchy sex and scandal, culture and politics, computing and more. But how do you access them? Are they censored? How do you read the messages, and post messages yourself? Written in plain English, this guide tells you everything you need to know to explore this lively and ever controversial side of the internet. Kye Valongo is a qualified teacher, computer analyst, internet journalist and former Education Officer for IBM.
1 84025 329 0

Education & Training on the Internet
An essential resource for students, teachers, and education providers
Laurel Alexander MIPD MICG

Confused by search engines? Fed up with floods of irrelevant information? This is a much-needed new guide to today's exploding new world of education and training online. It includes reviews of top web sites of every imaginable kind – for education and training providers, schools, colleges, universities, training centres, professional organisations, resource suppliers, individuals, business organisations and academic institutions. Whether you are planning to study online, or are planning the delivery of online education and training, you will find this a key resource. Laurel Alexander MIPD MICG is a qualified trainer, assessor and guidance specialist.
1 84025 346 0

Finding a Job on the Internet
Amazing new possibilities for jobseekers everywhere
Brendan Murphy BSc (Hons) MBA MBSC

Thinking of looking for a new job, or even a change of career? The internet is a great place to start your job search. In easy steps and plain English, this new guide explains how to find and use internet web sites and newsgroups to give you what you need. School, college and university leavers will find it invaluable for identifying suitable employers and getting expert help with CVs and job applications. The book will also be useful for career advisers and employers thinking of using the internet for recruitment purposes. Brendan Murphy BSc MBA MBSC teaches HNC in Computing, and lectures for the Open University.
1 84025 310 X – reprinted

Gardens & Gardening on the Internet
A practical handbook and reference guide to horticulture online
Judith & Graham Lawlor MA

Gardeners are often in need of specific information to help them in their projects, and the internet is proving an amazingly valuable new aid to modern gardening. This new book leads you quickly and painlessly to some amazing new gardening help lines, retail and wholesale suppliers, online clubs and societies, and web sites devoted to such topics as rare plants, water gardens, celebrity gardening, gardening holidays, and horticultural science. The book will be absolutely indispensable for all gardeners with access to the internet.
1 84025 313 4

Getting Connected to the Internet
A practical step-by-step guide for everyone
Ian Hosker

This book is intended for every PC owner who has not yet connected to the internet, but wants to do so provided they can feel confident about the process. It addresses all the questions commonly asked by the first-time subscriber. For example, what's the benefit of being online? What is an internet service provider (ISP)? What equipment do I need? What do I have to do, step-by-step? How do I send my first email? The book guides you carefully through all the initial stages. It shows how to get your computer ready, and how to load the required software from a CD. It explains how to create multiple email accounts, and perhaps most important of all, what to do if things don't go quite according to plan. Ian Hosker BEd(Hons) MSc is CVET Coordinator at the College of SS Mark & John in Plymouth.
1 84025 374 6

Getting Started on the Internet
A practical step-by-step guide for beginners
Kye Valongo

In plain English, this steps you through all the basics of the internet. It shows you how to obtain free access to the internet, how to set up your computer, how to look for information, and how to send and receive emails. It explains how to explore newsgroups and internet chat, how to protect your privacy online, and even how to create your own home page. Whether you want the internet for use at home, in education or in the workplace, this is the book for you, specially designed to get you up and running with the minimum fuss and bother. Kye Valongo is a qualified teacher, computer analyst, internet journalist and former Education Officer for IBM.
1 84025 321 5

Homes & Property on the Internet
A guide to 1000s of top web sites for buyers, sellers, owners, tenants, sharers, holiday makers & property professionals
Philip Harrison

Here is a guide to today's whole new world of homes and property services online. Here are web sites of every imaginable kind for estate agents, house builders, removal firms, decorators, town planners, architects and surveyors, banks and building societies, home shares, villa owners and renters, and property-related associations, pressure groups, newspapers and magazines. Whether you are planning to move house, or rent a holiday home, or locate property services in the UK or wider afield, this is the book for you – comprehensive and well-indexed to help you find what you want.
1 84025 335 5

Internet Explorer on the Internet
A step-by-step guide to using your browser
Kye Valongo

This book tells you all about Internet Explorer, the world's most popular and powerful browser. In practical steps, it explains how to use it for surfing the internet, how to send and read email messages using Outlook, and how to manage your electronic Address Book. Learn how to store selected web pages as Favourites (bookmarks). Discover how to disable irritating cookies. Find out how to control or delete sensitive computer files. If you are using Internet Explorer, or sharing access to a computer, this book will boost both your pleasure and protection when using the internet. Kye Valongo is a qualified teacher, computer analyst, internet journalist and former Education Officer for IBM.
1 84025 334 7

The Internet for Schools
A practical step-by-step guide for teachers, student teachers, parents and governors
Barry Thomas & Richard Williams

This title is aimed at teachers, student teachers, parents and school governors – in fact anyone interested in using the internet in primary and secondary education. The format is entertaining with key points highlighted. Each chapter is free-standing and should take no more than fifteen minutes to read. A major aim is to explain things in clear, non-technical and non-threatening language. There are detailed reviews of many key educational internet sites. Written by two experienced IT teachers, the book is UK focused, and contains typical examples and practical tasks that could be undertaken with students.
1 84025 302 9

The Internet for Students
Making the most of the new medium for study and fun
David Holland ACIB

Are you a student needing help with the internet to pursue your studies? Not sure where to start? – then this Internet Handbook is the one for you. It's up to date, full of useful ideas of places to visit on the internet, written in a clear and readable style, with plenty of illustrations and the minimum of jargon. It is the ideal introduction for all students who want to add interest to their studies, and make their finished work stand out, impressing lecturers and future employers alike. The internet is going to bring about enormous changes in modern life. As a student, make sure you are up to speed.
1 84025 306 1 – Reprinted

The Internet for Writers
Using the new medium to research, promote and publish your work
Nick Daws BSc(Hons)

This guide offers all writers with a complete introduction to the internet – how to master the basic skills, and how to use this amazing new medium to create, publish and promote your creative work. Would you like to broaden and speed up your research? Meet fellow writers, editors and publishers through web sites, newsgroups, or chat? Even publish your work on the internet for a potentially enormous new audience? Then this is the book you need, with all the practical starting points to get you going, step by step. The book is a selection of *The UK Good Book Guide*.
1 84025 308 8

Internet Skills for the Workplace
Empowering yourself for the digital age
Ian Hosker

The internet is fast becoming an essential tool in the workplace. This book is intended for everyone employed, or hoping to become employed, for any organisation that makes use of the internet in its daily activities. It helps you learn how to send, manage and reply to emails in a business setting, how to use a web browser, and how to research information using the internet. With its structured approach to learning specific new skills, the book makes an ideal companion for people taking City & Guilds and other training courses in internet competence. Ian Hosker BEd(Hons) MSc is CVET Coordinator at the College of SS Mark & John in Plymouth.
1 84025 328 2

Other Internet Handbooks...

Law & Lawyers on the Internet
An essential guide and resource for legal practitioners
Stephen Hardy JP LLB PhD

Following the Woolf Reforms, efficient research and communication will be the key to future legal life. This handbook will meet the needs of solicitors, barristers, law students, public officials, community groups and consumers who are seeking guidance on how to access and use the major legal web sites and information systems available to them on the internet. It includes expert site reviews on law associations, law firms, case law and court reporting, European legal institutions, government, legal education and training, publishers, the courts and branches of the law. Don't leave for court without it! Stephen Hardy JP LLB PhD teaches law at the University of Manchester Business School.
1 84025 345 2

Marketing Your Business on the Internet (2nd edition)
A practical step-by-step guide for all business owners and managers
Sara Edlington

Written by someone experienced in marketing on the internet from its earliest days, this practical book will show you step-by-step how to make a success of marketing your organisation on the internet. Discover how to find a profitable on-line niche, know which ten essential items to have on your web site, how to keep visitors returning again and again, how to secure valuable on- and off-line publicity for your organisation, and how to build your brand online. The internet is set to create phenomenal new marketing opportunities – make sure you are ready to win your share.
1 84025 364 9 (2nd edition)

Medicine & Health on the Internet
A practical guide to online advice, treatments, doctors and support groups
Sarah Wilkinson

In the last couple of years, thousands of new health and medical web sites have been launched on the internet. Do you want to find out about a specialist treatment or therapy? Do you want to contact a support group or clinician online, or perhaps just get the answer to a simple question? Don't get lost using search engines. Whether you are a patient, relative, carer, doctor, health administrator, medical student or nurse, this book will lead you quickly to all the established web sites you need – help lines, support groups, hospitals, clinics and hospices, health insurance and pharmaceutical companies, treatments, suppliers, professional bodies, journals, and more.
1 84025 337 1

Naming a Web Site on the Internet
How to choose, register and protect the right domain name for your web site
Graham Jones BSc (Hons)

Would you like to obtain a proper domain name for your own web site, for example 'dot.com' or 'dot.co.uk'? Perhaps you have a name in mind, but are not sure how to register it. Do you know the rules which govern the naming of web sites? This valuable handbook explains just how to choose and register your own 'domain name' on the world wide web. The official rules are clearly explained, with lots of practical examples to help you. There are many places you can apply for a domain name and a bewildering array of prices and conditions. This book provides a clear step-by-step guide through the maze. It also explains how to protect your domain names, where to 'host' them, and how to move them from one machine to another. The rush is on – act now to register and protect the names you want.
1 84025 359 2

Personal Finance on the Internet
Your complete online guide to savings, investment, loans, mortgages, pensions, insurance and all aspects of personal finance
Graham Jones BSc(Hons)

For many people the internet is now the preferred means of managing their personal finances. But how do you do it? Where can you check out financial products and services on the internet? How secure is it, and what are the risks? Step-by-step this book explains what you need to run your finances on the internet, where to find financial information, managing your bank account online, getting credit via the internet, checking out mortgages, saving your money online, buying and selling stocks and shares online, arranging your pensions and insurance online, paying taxes, and much more. Graham Jones BSc(Hons) is an Associate Lecturer with the Open University and author of 17 books on internet and business topics.
1 84025 320 7

Shops & Shopping on the Internet
A practical guide to online stores, catalogues, retailers and shopping malls
Kathy Lambert

In the last couple of years, thousands of shops and stores have been launched on the internet. But what are they like? Where can you find your favourite brands and stores? What about deliveries from suppliers in the UK or overseas? Can you safely pay by credit card? Don't get stuck in the internet traffic! This carefully structured book will take you quickly to all the specialist stores, virtual shopping malls, and online catalogues of your choice. You will be able to compare prices, and shop till you drop for books, magazines, music, videos, clothes, holidays, electrical goods, games and toys, wines, and a vast array of other goods and services.
1 84025 327 4

Studying English on the Internet
An A to Z guide to useful electronic resources freely available on the internet
Wendy Shaw BSc(Hons)

Written by a university researcher, this new guide has been specially collated for the internet user of all levels in the discipline of English. Whether you are a student, teacher, tutor or lecturer, this is the guide for you. It offers a clear and graphical presentation of web sites and electronic resources on the internet for both teaching and research purposes. The A-Z format makes it easy to pick out an author or electronic text centre from the bulleted list. Hundreds of key gateway web sites for English Studies are reviewed in this valuable course companion.
1 84025 317 7

Studying Law on the Interent
How to use the internet for learning and study, exams and career development
Stephen Hardy JP LLB PhD

Are you studying law at college or university, or as a distance learner? Do you have internet access? Computers and the internet are becoming ever more important in both legal learning and practice today. The internet in particular is a rich legal resource for barristers, solicitors, legal executives and officials alike. This handbook meets the needs of law students wanting quick access to the major relevant legal web sites and legal information systems available over the internet. Use this book to expand your knowledge, develop your skills, and greatly improve your career prospects. Stephen Hardy JP LLB PhD teaches law at the University of Manchester Business School.
1 84025 370 3

Travel & Holidays on the Internet
The amazing new world of online travel services, information, prices, reservations, timetables, bookings and more
Graham Jones BSc(Hons)

Thinking of checking out flights to Europe or America, or booking a package holiday? The internet is the best place to start. In easy steps and plain English, this book explains how to find and use the web to locate the travel and holiday information you need. You can view the insides of hotels, villas and even aeroplanes, quickly compare costs and services, and make your reservations and bookings securely online. You'll be amazed at how much more you'll find with the help of this remarkable book. Graham Jones BSc(Hons) is an Associate Lecturer with the Open University and author of 17 books on internet and business topics.
1 84025 325 8

Using Credit Cards on the Internet
A practical step-by-step guide for all cardholders and retailers
Graham Jones BSc(Hons)

Are you worried about using credit cards on the internet? This valuable book shows you how to avoid trouble and use your 'virtual plastic' in complete safety over the internet. It contains all the low-down on security, practical tips to make sure that all your credit card dealings are secure, and advice on where to find credit cards with extra 'web protection'. If you are running a business on the internet, it also explains how to set up a 'merchant account' so that customers can safely pay you using their credit cards. The book is complete with a guide to the best web sites on credit card usage. Graham Jones BSc(Hons) is an Associate Lecturer with the Open University and author of 17 books on internet and business topics.
1 84025 349 5

Where to Find It on the Internet (2nd edition)
Your complete guide to search engines, portals, databases, yellow pages & other internet reference tools
Kye Valongo

Here is a valuable basic reference guide to hundreds of carefully selected web sites for everyone wanting to track down information on the internet. Don't waste time with fruitless searches – get to the sites you want, fast. This book provides a complete selection of the best search engines, online databases, directories, libraries, people finders, yellow pages, portals, and other powerful research tools. A recent selection of *The Good Book Guide*, and now in a new edition, this book will be an essential companion for all internet users, whether at home, in education, or in the workplace. Kye Valongo is a qualified teacher, computer analyst, internet journalist and former Education Officer for IBM.
1 84025 369 X – 2nd edition

Wildlife & Conservation on the Internet
An essential guide to environmental resources online
Kate Grey BSc(Hons)

Are you interested in the future of our natural heritage? Perhaps you are a student or teacher of environmental studies, or with a job in this responsible area? Here is a unique guide to wildlife trusts, official and public organisations, coastal and marine web sites, nature reserves, zoos, national parks, and thousands more online resources. With its expert reviews, this timely book is essential reference for town and country dwellers, officials and planners, conservationists, and everyone interested in environmental issues. It is also a valuable resource for primary and secondary schools and teachers, and college lecturers, using the internet for educational purposes.
1 84025 318 5